ÆSTHETIC PRINCIPLES

BY

HENRY RUTGERS MARSHALL, M.A.

AUTHOR OF "PAIN, PLEASURE, AND ÆSTHETICS"

New York

MACMILLAN AND CO.

AND LONDON

1895

COPYRIGHT, 1895,
BY MACMILLAN AND CO.

Norwood Press:
J. S. Cushing & Co. — Berwick & Smith.
Norwood, Mass., U.S.A.

PREFACE.

ONE of the kindly critics of my book on *Pain, Pleasure, and Æsthetics* has compared the task of its reading with the effort required in walking over a ploughed field after a heavy rain; although in the end, I am glad to say, he finds the labour healthful, and looks back upon the effort with pleasure. I have thought it worth while to try to show to such readers a way across this ploughed field which will not involve so much arduous labour on their part; and I think this possible because the explorer of a field is often able to guide others with ease in a path already trodden and therefore familiar, being able in places to take a straighter course than that at first necessary, because it is no longer needful to search for the path.

In this small volume I do not attempt to cover the whole subject discussed in my former work above referred to; but I do attempt to sketch out the results which are of greatest interest and of most practical value in reference to the study of Æsthetics.

If this book meet the eye of some scientific psychologist, I must beg him to remember that it is written for less critical readers, and that I have at times, in the interests of clearness, abandoned the strictest accuracy in verbal expression where this accuracy would have involved too technical a phraseology. I must beg him to judge me rather by my larger work.

The reader who is not a psychologist may find the second chapter tedious; if so, it may be passed over without loss of the drift of the argument so far as it relates to æsthetic problems; still, I hope he will not pass it over without a trial.

This book, already under consideration, was hastened to completion in consequence of the kind request by the Trustees of Columbia College, New York, that I deliver a course of lectures upon the subject of Æsthetics under their auspices. The reader who happens to have been present at those lectures, delivered during November and December, 1894, will notice that the substance of them is contained in the pages that follow, although the topics are here somewhat differently arranged and are more fully treated.

NEW YORK, February, 1895.

CONTENTS.

ix

CHAPTER V.

CHAPTER VI.

ÆSTHETIC PRINCIPLES.

CHAPTER I.

THE OBSERVER'S STANDPOINT. I.

The Field of Æsthetics.

THE word "Æsthetics" is one which is to
be used, in what follows, with a very broad
signification, to refer to the whole realm of
Beauty. Judged etymologically, the word
might seem properly to have a somewhat
narrower meaning than that which we thus
give to it, for it was derived by Baumgarten
from the Greek αἰσθητικός, meaning *appre-
hended by the senses ;* and it was used by him
to describe the Beautiful as a whole, only
because he thought the Beautiful could be
explained in some manner as arising from

the obscure perception of sense impressions or of the relations between them. Although his narrow view must be discarded, the word has become so firmly fixed with the broader meaning that there is no reason why it should not be used, as it is employed very generally to-day, and as we shall here use it, to indicate the whole field of Beauty.

Æsthetics, then, is the science of the Beautiful; and during the whole of this study we must not allow ourselves to forget this broad meaning attached to the word. It is meant to cover not only Beauty proper, but also the Sublime and the Ludicrous, which are states sometimes separated entirely from Beauty, although generally acknowledged to be closely allied to it. As the mental effects of the Sublime and Ludicrous are more evanescent than those produced by what we call the Beautiful, we shall naturally find ourselves discussing almost entirely the problems of Beauty proper.

Æsthetics, too, must take account of the

Beautiful in nature as well as in the works of man; for the thrill with which each affects us is the same. This is recognized unwittingly in the habitual emphasis of the *imitation of nature* in the practical work of the artists and in the teaching of many philosophical writers from Aristotle's [1] time to this day. But there is a tendency, of late especially, to speak of art and of its beauties apart from the beauties in nature, a mode of thought too likely to carry one into discussions about special skill, or to limit ones view by an emphasis of some special art which is held to be higher than another. The hierarchy of the arts is a matter to be determined finally by metaphysical conditions, and one with which we need not concern ourselves here. For us, in this our most general view, separation of the arts is altogether out of place; all of them must be

---

[1] M. Bosanquet thinks this emphasis of Imitation is not properly attributed to Aristotle, as is done by many of his commentators.

gathered together without exclusion of any one, and their effects must be considered in conjunction with the effects produced by nature in bringing to us the impression of Beauty.

The reader then will find me using the words "Æsthetics" and "Beauty" and "Art" and "Artist" in the widest possible way. Even if we ourselves get no æsthetic delight from a given impression, we must take it for granted that the impression is æsthetic for others, if they tell us that the object considered is beautiful for them, either by speech or in other mode than speech, viz., by their action in relation to it. The word "Art" is commonly used to cover the whole realm of æsthetic endeavour, and I know of no other word as good as "Artist," that can be used to indicate the æsthetic worker in each and all of the varied fields in which beauty is of moment. I shall use the word thus although it is often employed to refer to painters and draughtsmen only.

So much for our broad use of terms. Now let us take a different standpoint; let us consider a *distinction* which seems to me to be of importance.

There are two ways in which we may look upon æsthetic problems; we may consider, first, the nature of the *impression* made upon the observer, and, second, the nature of the *instinct* that leads to the production of the art-work.

In my study of what has been done in the past by thoughtful men in this department, I find, very frequently, obscurities of one kind or another which seem to me to be caused by the failure to distinguish between these two ways of looking at the subject that we have before us.

We have, then, two different standpoints: first, the "Observer's Standpoint," relating to the field of Impression, and, second, the "Artist's Standpoint," which deals with the Art Instinct. In one sense the "Observer's Standpoint" is of wider interest than the

"Artist's Standpoint," because the former brings us into direct communion with nature, which we have seen furnishes us so important a part of our æsthetic field; whilst the latter, the view which emphasizes the impulse to creative work in art, is bound to nature less directly, but on the other hand gains in width and importance in that it cannot be cut away altogether from the "Observer's Standpoint"; for the artist must alternately follow his creative instinct and become the observer and critic of his own work.

In this chapter we shall take the standpoint of the observer; we shall consider Beauty as impressing itself upon us, and we shall ask what are the characteristics which produce this effective impression.

As soon as man learns to feel the value of beauty in nature and in art, he is most naturally led to consider the æsthetic failure of the great mass of objects that surround him.

As naturally does he long to find some means
by which he may infuse this loved beauty
into his surroundings; some principle by the
application of which he may destroy ugliness;
for how glorious, how noble, it would be, will
he say, could all things that impress us be
beautiful whichever way we turn!

So it happens that we find thinkers from
the earliest times making research for the
principles of beauty. Few persons, indeed,
who have not undertaken the serious study
of Æsthetics from a historical standpoint
have any notion of the enormous amount
of human thought of the higher type that
has been given to this subject. And
surely we may look forward with keen-
est anticipation to a renewal of the quest.
For if the pathway of our predecessors be
filled with signs of failure, surely the end
to which we strive is shown to be worthy
of our labour by the large number of important thinkers who have turned their attention to strictly æsthetic problems.

It is most natural for man, when attention is first given to such a problem as the one we are to consider, to turn to the objects which are impressing him, and to seek for some special characteristic in the objects themselves, some objective quality, which shall account for the special impression gained.

To explain what I mean, let us suppose that we had discovered that many beautiful objects were *round;* and had concluded that roundness was the element essential to beauty. This, of course, is not true; but if it were true we should have in roundness what I speak of here as an objective quality; we always think of roundness as inhering in objects; we project roundness into the outer world of objective things. To attempt to identify beauty with some one or more such objective qualities is, I say, in line with the most natural movement of thought; for we all have an inveterate habit of objectifying every mental state.

The Greek philosophers had but begun to

see dimly the subjective aspect of things; and it is not surprising to find that Aristotle recorded a list of objective qualities, such as *order*, *symmetry*, a *certain magnitude*, upon which he made the beautiful dependent. It is evident, however, upon the most superficial view, that beauty, in the wider sense in which we are considering it, cannot be bound within any such narrow limits. Few other thinkers have dared to list the qualities of the object which determined its beauty; but this is, in my opinion, not because the method has not occurred to them, but because they have become so soon convinced of the futility of the attempt to gain satisfactory result by this means.

The most persuasive effort in the direction of objective observation is that made by the Idealist philosophers, who claim to find in beautiful objects some fixed Universal or Absolute which determines its beauty. This view has held strongly from Plato's time to our own; but the great difficulty in the way of the acceptance of any of the many suggested schemes of Absolute or Universal Æsthetics is that they one and all fail to account for those differences of standard which have led the bewildered man to cry *de gustibus non est disputandum*.

If there be a fixed Universal or Absolute Beauty, we may well ask, How does it happen that you and I do not both see it in the same object? Is this due, as Bergmann has suggested, to real differences in the object seen, which we mistakenly think to be alike for each of us? Then surely we have gained no fundamental principle.

Is it due to differences of our own development, as Lotze held; so that you, my reader, see a beauty in an object that I, in my less developed condition, cannot grasp? This will indeed enable us to account for more or less of beauty, in proportion to our state of development; but not, so far as I can see, for the fact that what I in my childhood held to be beautiful, I now find to be positively ugly;

nor for the fact that what I call' beautiful in my less developed state, you with your higher cultivation find to be distinctly bad in æsthetic quality, the object thus not merely lacking something of a special characteristic, but really possessing its opposite.

There is another difficulty about this notion of a fixed Absolute of beauty ; viz., that it fails to make comprehensible the fact which is well recognized, that some men who are very sensitive to art in some of its developments are utterly incapable of appreciating its glories in other developments of a diverse kind. The musician perhaps cares little for paintings; the sculptor perhaps nothing for music. But if beauty were a fixed objective thing that we were striving to reach, or to gain a glimpse of, then if the glimpse were obtained in the direction of the development of one art, there seems to be no reason why the capacity to recognize this beauty in connection with other arts should, in any case, be lacking.

Now there is no objection to the objective view itself, and we might well adopt it, if it led us anywhere; but investigations on this line have failed us in the past, and there seems little reason to hope that they will aid us greatly in the future; and, in truth, the beautiful is too egotistic, too clearly beautiful *for me*, to be considered as inhering in the object itself, and I wish now to ask the reader to turn to the *subjective* view: to consider his or her mental experience at the moment when he or she is impressed by the beauty of an object.

Of subjective views there are many; theories dependent upon attempts to analyze the special state of mind into which we are thrown as we contemplate a work of art or some beautiful object in nature.

There have been men who have emphasized the importance of the kind of *sensations* received when we are thus impressed. Of Baumgarten we have spoken. In our generation Grant Allen stands as the special expo-

nent of such doctrine. There have been men
who have emphasized the strictly *emotional*
conditions aroused during the impression; *e.g.*,
Alison, James Mill, Burke, Guyau. There
have been others without number who have
thought that the *intellectual* forms of mental
life arising as the result of the impression,
were all important. Rationalism and formalism have developed into mysticism; which
is itself a form of æsthetic experience, that
leads one to cling blindly to the doctrines
involved even if their ground be shown
to be inadequate.

We cannot stop here to examine these
doctrines in detail. The interested reader
may refer to my fuller work, *Pain, Pleasure, and Æsthetics*, for discussion of these
special theories. I think it is there shown
that they all fail in their attempts at limi-
tation; and it is generally agreed to-day by
the best thinkers that all elements of our
mental life, whether sensational, or emotional,
or intellectual, or of will, are exercised in the

state of mind which gives us the notion of the beautiful. This implies that there is some common *subjective quality* attachable to all these mental states which is of the very essence of æsthetic phenomena.

To indicate what I mean, let us suppose that we had noticed that a certain grade of *intensity* of Sensation was always beautiful, and that we had extended this thought to Emotion, Intellect, and Will. Then we should be able to claim that *intensity* was of the essence of beauty. Of course this is not true; but if it were, we should here have the essence of beauty placed in a *subjective quality*; for intensity is clearly not in the *object* (although its cause may be), but it is distinctly *in us*. Now such a quality as we are in search of I think we have in *pleasure*, which is clearly a subjective quality, and one that is attached to Sensation, to Emotion, to Intellect, and to Will. To this special characteristic of the æsthetic mental impression I wish now to draw the reader's particular attention.

Thinkers of varied authority and of all schools, from Aristotle down, have acknowledged explicitly or implicitly the connection between beauty and pleasure. Indeed, we might consider this a commonplace but for the fact that we find doubt in the matter in the minds of many art workers, and theoretical opposition on the part of certain formalistic thinkers who distinctly deny the importance of the connection: Von Hartman, for instance, takes this position. On the other hand, it is not difficult to find authorities from Epicurus to Hume whose statements may be interpreted as decisive expressions of the view for which I argue; and there are some few men, the noted Fechner for example, who distinctly base Æsthetics upon the science of pleasure. But at the very beginning of this consideration, from the hedonic standpoint, we are met by the evident fact that, while all æsthetic phenomena are pleasurable, not all pleasures are held to be æsthetic. It seems, therefore, that it will be necessary for us to indicate the special kinds of pleasures which are æsthetic, if we are to make pleasure fundamental to Æsthetics; if we are to treat the science of the beautiful as a branch of hedonics, — the science of pleasure. The problem before us then may be stated in the form of this question: What are the bounds of the æsthetic within the hedonic field?

We must, however, avoid making too much of the separation of which we have just been speaking: the distinctions, indeed, are too easily emphasized, and the connections too often lost sight of by theoretical writers. But if one examine the literary work of art critics, and the more or less philosophic and scientific writings that deal with the facts of Æsthetics rather than its theory, one will find little more than descriptions of pleasure-getting coupled with attempts to arrange this pleasure-getting in a logical way. If, on the other hand, one examine the writings of those who have studied most closely the psychology of pleasure, he will find æsthetic phenomena treated altogether as the best recognized data of the science of pleasure, exactly as the simplest sense-pleasures are used. Evidently then it is the connection between the two sets of phenomena that we must ever. bear in mind throughout what follows. A suggestive argument in favour of this connection is found if we consider any average complex æsthetic object, which, if we notice its characteristics with care, we find to be very wide in its effects upon us, and yet embodying certain special elements that appear emphatically pleasant. If now we eliminate in thought the pleasurable elements one by one, we find that while in the main the object does not change its mass, its æsthetic quality gradually disappears. We may acknowledge still that the object has a right to be *named* æsthetic, because of the opinions of others and because of our own judgments in the past; but for ourselves, at the time, it has lost all that makes

c

it worthy of being called by so honourable a name. We are all familiar with the fact that an object which but a moment ago was æsthetic for us, may become unæsthetic by the degradation into indifference or positive painfulness of the special elements which were giving us pleasure. The suggestion of a painful association with some essential element in an art complex will for all time reduce for us the æsthetic value of the whole form. One special mountain of great natural charm has lost for me all of its impressiveness, because a light-hearted companion once compared its autumn colouring with that of "corned-beef hash." It is by a similar process that the average art critic makes and unmakes æsthetic objects for the masses: degrading one object of real merit by ridicule, always thereafter to be associated with it; giving a fallacious value to another by the unmerited praise lavished upon it.

It thus appears very clear, I think, that the state of æsthetic impression is most closely bound to the state of pleasure.

But if the connection be so intimate, and the æsthetic be no more than a part of the pleasure-field, one would say on the spur of the moment that it should be no difficult task, in some rough way, to mark off that part of the field which is æsthetic from that which is not. The task, however, is not nearly so easy as we expect to find it.

In my larger work I have shown that we cannot separate the æsthetic by the cutting off of *sensational* pleasures, a view held by no less an authority than Kant, but opposed by other eminently authoritative observers, *e.g.*, Lotze and Lipps. In fact, there is no attempt whatever to cut off any but the so-called "lower pleasures," and these, after all, are judged by ethical, and not by hedonic standards.

Nor can we cut off the *emotional* nor the *intellectual;* nor again the *active* pleasures, as Grant Allen would have us do; nor can we limit the æsthetic to pleasures of a *moral* or *spiritual* type; nor to those attendant upon

the use of the *imagination*. Neither will
limitations to *immediacy* of pleasure effect,
nor to *width* of pleasurable impression, suffice
us. All of these theories have been advanced
and stoutly defended, but have shown fatal
weaknesses upon close examination.

We are brought, indeed, to see that in æsthetic impressions there are no pleasures
whatever that cannot become part and parcel
of the pleasurable æsthetic effect. The ordinary use of language confirms this view, for
notice how freely we use the word "beautiful"
to describe the most commonplace of pleasures. The child calls his sweets beautiful.
The schoolgirl talks of having a "beautiful
time" at an entertainment, and the patholo-
gist speaks of a beautiful preparation of some
cancerous tissue. The Germans use "schön"
in much the same way; and so it is with the
more varied expressions used by the Frenchman.

Now if no pleasure of impression can be
cut away from the rest and held to be non-

æsthetic, then it is apparent that the distinction between non-æsthetic pleasures and æsthetic pleasures cannot arise by difference between pleasures in *impression*, but must arise in the process of judging about them; in other words, it is only when we come to ask ourselves whether some special impression that we call a pleasure is æsthetic or not, that we find ourselves making the distinction between the two fields in an act of judgment. This is an important distinction and must not be lost sight of; we shall refer to it again.

But at this point I wish to refer to one special emphasis considered in the first part of this chapter. We there observed that a very large number of authoritative thinkers, not to speak of lesser lights, have looked upon beauty as an objective quality; as something fixed; an Absolute or Universal. This they could not have done had they not in introspection found an appearance of stability, of fixity, in connection with æsthetic phenomena; and the question at once arises, may not the difference between non-æsthetic and æsthetic pleasures be determined by the permanence of those which are called æsthetic.

But this can scarcely be true, for pleasures are notably evanescent, and we all recognize this fact. From childhood to mature age, we are found deploring the loss at one moment of a pleasure we were but lately experiencing; the ephemeral nature of pleasure is the theme of the pessimist, and a fact the optimist strives to make intelligent.

If, however, we are compelled to admit that it is impossible to sift out some certain class of pleasures which are permanent, and identify them with what is æsthetic; still it does appear possible, on the other hand, to arrive at a relatively permanent *field* of pleasure in various ways, although experience and theory both deny the possibility of there being any permanency of any specific pleasure.

In the first place we should find, if we stopped to study the nature of pleasure, that the more powerful the pleasures are the more quickly their apparent strength wanes; that the rapidity of the waning is much less apparent when the pleasures are of low degree. If, then, we can hold a large number of lighter pleasures together by some process of *summation,* if we may use the term, by adding them together as it were, we ought to be able to reach something that would be less evanescent than any simple pleasure itself could be.

That this *summation of pleasures* is possible, is evident to all of us when we think of certain sensations that yield to us no noticeable delight unless they are, at one and the same time, widely felt. We may touch our finger-tip to satin or fur with none of the noticeable pleasure that we find when the whole surface of our hand is passed over the same satin or fur, by which latter action we bring innumerable touch-nerve terminals into activity at one time. We may not notice the application of heat to any single spot on our body to be at all agreeable, but if we stand before a fire on a cool day the sum of all the stimulations of the many heat-nerve terminals gives us one of the most voluminous pleasures we can obtain. Now I think that if we observe our experience of what is beautiful in natural objects and in many types of art work, we shall find that a great part of the pleasurable effect produced is due to the massing together of many delights, which individually are not notably vivid. We will at once recognize this truth, if we consider the varied pleasant stimuli of colour, of line, of form, that are involved in our perception of a beautiful scene in nature; and so it is with the pictorial arts which directly follow nature's leadings. We find the same thing strongly marked in the field of music, especially in its later complex development; there we depend largely for our æsthetic delight, any one will admit, upon the fulness of the background of aural pleasures, less distinct in themselves than those called forth by the melodic progressions. The same fulness of pleasure background may be discerned in all of the greatest art works.

Looking in another direction, we find that *an appearance of permanent pleasure may be obtained, if we are able to bring about the cessation of activities that are pleasant before their pleasure wanes and is transformed into pain;* such waning of pleasure, and transformation into pain, occurring in all directions under continuous stimulation. To explain what I mean let us take the example of sugar. We are not compelled to eat sugar as a matter of diet; and we take it only so far as we like to do so, and we stop eating it just as soon as our liking begins to fail us. Consequently we naturally think of the taste of sugar as being pleasant, and Mr. Herbert Spencer has actually been led to say in some one of his writings, that sugar is a taste that can never be experienced in any disagreeable phase. But I think a little experimentation will prove to any one that, if he keep on eating sugar long enough, its taste will become exceedingly unpleasant to him. This is proven in truth by the fact that the shop-girls in candy shops are not put under restriction. If the candy before them continued to bring pleasure with its sweetness, some restriction to the eating of it would have to be adopted by their employers.

Now let us see whether this principle is one which artists naturally adopt. It is at once apparent that the stimuli obtained from the beautiful objects created by man are under control; that their special impressions may be withdrawn from consciousness at our will so soon as they begin to pall upon us. It is most important, if we are to retain the notion of beauty in any special direction, that we avoid any continuous attention to the special impressions involved, after they have sunk to indifference or have begun to tire us.

To make this clearer let us illustrate this point to some extent. As our musical programmes are arranged there is at times, for some people, difficulty in avoiding this tiredness, although, as we shall presently see, this difficulty is, to a great degree, compensated for; but the arts that are dependent upon the organs of sight have here a pre-eminent advantage, for a simple turning of the head or eyes, or closing of the eyelids, will enable us to avoid continuation of the stimulation, this protective action indeed taking place automatically just as soon as a glimmering of painfulness begins to appear. With the ear, however, stimulation cannot be controlled by any such simple movements. We must take ourselves bodily from the concert-hall, or else we can only avoid the sound-painfulness, if it is beginning to arise, by the stopping of the ears, or less fully, but more graciously, distract our attention by conversation, or still more graciously by watching those around us. In fact, what we may call the social difficulties that go with control of the stimuli to the ear, affect our theatre-goers and music-lovers not a little: we learn by experience that others will watch us at the theatre and opera house, and this goes far to account for the fact that we all, but women especially, feel impelled to wear our finest clothes and to make ourselves as attractive as possible, when going to hear play or opera, at which conversational distractions are less allowable than in the picture-gallery, where we find dress much less considered. The inveterate habit of the eating of sweets at the plays is also a means of distraction, which has been in vogue ever since the time of the Greek supremacy. Here perhaps I may be allowed to make a suggestion to the musical artist. The skilled musician is far too apt to misjudge the capacity of the audience he calls together; too often does he forget the danger of tiring his audience with music which they cannot comprehend

so well as he does himself. Many music-
lovers would attend symphonic concerts who
now do not, were it not that under existing
social conditions they are unable to avoid
the disagreeableness which goes with the
necessity of listening after they have become
tired. The German habit of listening to
music whilst smoking and eating and drink-
ing is much more rational for the average
audience; for thus the hearer retains his
ability to change his field of attention without disturbance to his neighbours.

But there is still another means by which
*an apparent pleasure permanence may be ob-
tained: viz., by the shifting of the field of
mental elements;* by the turning of our attention successively to different subjects or different qualities of the same subject, so that
as one set of pleasures fades, another set will
arise to take its place. That this kind of
pleasure permanence belongs to all æsthetic
objects I think will be agreed. In examin-
ing a picture or a piece of sculpture we find

ourselves constantly changing our point of
view, either actually, physically, or more often
merely mentally. But it is here that the
Arts of the Ear have a decided advantage
over the Arts of the Eye, for the playwright
or musical composer has it in his power to
stop at will one series of effects and substi-
tute for it another series, and this process he
may continue almost indefinitely, in a way
that is impossible for the pictorial artist as
he at present limits himself: it is not impossible that some day, through the development
of the panoramic art, this power may be
added to the resources of him who appeals
directly to the eye only.

I think my reader will now agree to this:
that while we have found that there are no
pleasures which are not evanescent; on the
other hand, we have discovered that there are
pleasure-fields that are relatively permanent.
But we have seen above that it is in the
act of judgment that we separate non-æs-

thetic from æsthetic pleasures. It seems but
a step, therefore, to the fundamental hypothesis that I shall uphold, which is this: that,
as we saw in the early part of the chapter,
all that is pleasure at the time makes part
of the æsthetic *impression;* but only that
is *judged* to be æsthetic which appears to
be permanently pleasant in revival, *i.e.* in
the reflection that is necessary in an act of
judgment.

That which in memory appears thus to be
a stable pleasure, we call æsthetic; what is
indifferent in contemplation, we tolerate only
as an adjunct; what is painful in reflection,
we cast out of the æsthetic field entirely.
We do not always judge a work to be non-
æsthetic because of a painful element in its
revival, but we exclude that element as non-
æsthetic.

But what shall we say of those so-called
"pleasures" that are judged to be non-æsthetic? I hold that in the recall necessary
to judgment they are not pleasures at all;

they are revived mental elements to which the name "pleasure" persistently clings, although the actual pleasure has gone out of them entirely, the name clinging because of the strong pleasant emphasis of the original state.

Thus the so-called "lower pleasures" have been powerful pleasures in our original experience, but in memory the experience is not pleasurable, or else it is so closely bound up with restrictive painfulness connected with our ethical life that we do not find the experience as a whole to be part of our relatively permanent pleasure-field; hence we call these states non-æsthetic, although we still call them pleasures because the name was so closely attached to the original experience, of which the revival only is considered in our æsthetic judgment. Before we attempt to illustrate this view, we must pause to consider to some extent the nature of pleasure and pain, which we shall do in the next chapter.

CHAPTER II.

Pleasure and Pain.

No one of my readers, I believe, will regret that the study of the fundamental æsthetic problem leads us to fix our attention upon Pleasure.

There is certainly no more fascinating subject of investigation among the many which appeal to the psychologist than that of Pleasure and its correlate Pain; but it is a subject about which the psychological world is not at all at ease; it is the centre just now of polemical oppositions, for it has been until very lately sadly neglected by the present generation of psychologists, who, with new methods and clearer observation, have developed what they somewhat egotis-

tically call the "new psychology." I shall
not ask my reader here to enter the field
of contention, but shall rather beg him for
a moment, and I assure him for only a
moment, to stand with me aside from the
polemical turmoil and notice the drift of
opinion.

What are the characteristics of pleasures
and pains by which we are enabled to relate them to the rest of our conscious life?

Let us consider first the answer of common sense to the question. In every-day
conversation we find ourselves grouping pleasures and pains together; they are different
states; states in a sense exclusive of one
another, and yet in some way so 'bound
together that we can scarcely speak of them
except in one breath. This is due, doubtless, to the fact that, in common experience,
conscious states fade from pleasantness into
painfulness with no distinct line of demar-
cation between the two, and often with no
change in the mental elements, except the

pleasure and pain themselves. It is evident, therefore, that it will be logically and psychologically improper to group pleasure and pain apart from one another, the one under one class of mental phenomena, and the other under another class.

Still this improper course is exactly what we do find adopted by plain people in everyday conversation, and by more thoughtful men when they speak incautiously. We are very likely to speak of pains as sensational, and of pleasures as emotional. But sensations and emotions are certainly two very diverse species of mental phenomena. *Sensations* are those mental states that are determined, acknowledgedly in all but some pathological cases, by the action of some special organs terminating in the bodily surfaces, and brought into activity by special environmental conditions: for example, Sight, Hearing, Touch, Pressure, Taste, Smell, Heat, Cold. *Emotions*, on the other hand, as we shall see in the next chapter, are the mental side of certain reflex reactions of the whole nervous organism, dependent upon the perception of external objects. Such states are Joy, Sorrow, Love, Fear, Surprise, etc.

A critical examination leads us to see that pleasures and pains cannot be *sensations* for many reasons which I cannot detail here; but it is to be noted that there has been no natural claim that *pleasures* are sensations, the claim being limited to *pains*, which are most notable as produced apparently by the same actions, which involve special forms of sensation; viz., by blows, cuts, crushings, burnings, etc.

On the other hand, a critical examination shows us that pleasures and pains cannot be *emotions*, for pleasures and pains are not called out by the perception of external objects as emotions are, nor can they for a moment be looked upon as the mental coincidents of reflex reactions of our whole nervous organism, as in the case of the emotions. These facts taken together, with the close connection between the words "pleasure" and "pain" first noted, would naturally lead us to the conclusion that pleasure and pain are in some way connected both with sensations and with emotions, and that pain is especially emphatic in sensational consciousness, while pleasure is most prominently noted in the life of emotion.

The importance of the wide connection thus noted is emphasized when we consider that purely intellectual operations and acts of will, both of which are naturally separated from sensation and emotion alike, still somehow have pleasure and pain attached to them also. We have what we call intellectual pleasures and pains, and there is no doubt that in common speech there is indicated the conception of a close connection between pleasure-pain and action of will.

The general connection with all fields of mental activity thus acknowledged by us in every-day life may be accounted for on at least one of three grounds.

1st. It has been held that *pleasure and pain are the fundamental elements* out of which all else of mental life has been developed. This view is fascinating to any one of a philosophic trend, because of its monistic leanings; but evidence in favour of it fails, and the view has not been defended by any man who is acknowledged to be a master of the first order.

2d. The explanation of the facts, which may in a sense be said to be orthodox in our day, is that of Kant and his successors, viz., that *pleasure and pain are a mental series, sui generis,* brought into activity in some occult way by all other forms of mental action. This hypothesis was constructed originally to fill out a gap in metaphysical systemization, and a critical examination of it, from a psychological standpoint, shows that the evidence in its favour is exceedingly weak.

3d. There is another theory, however, which seems to account for the facts more satisfactorily, viz., *that pleasures and pains are qualities either of which, under the proper conditions, may belong to any element of consciousness, and one of which must in any case belong to each element.*

This hypothesis seems to meet the psychological objections which arise in opposition to the other hypotheses suggested above, and is favoured by much evidence reached in many directions, which I cannot detail here.

Now if we turn away from common sense to a more scientific classification, we find ourselves led to the same view. If we examine the studies of psychologists and philosophers in the past, in reference to this subject, we find in each case that the theory defended is based upon an emphasis of some special form of pleasure or pain, and an attempt to relate all other pleasures and pains to this special form, which, for one reason or another, has become emphasized in the mental life of the theorist. We are thus led to see that in general there are two wide classes of pleasures and two wide classes of pains, and none which cannot be included in these four classes.

1st. There are pains and also pleasures connected with *cessation of activities*.

The pains of restriction, of disappointment, of despair.

The pleasures of rest after strain.

2d. There are pains and also pleasures connected with *active functioning*.

The pains of excess, of strain, of hypernormal and destructive influences upon the tissues.

The pleasures of vigorous exercise.

But it is not difficult to show that unless we are to attack the most generally accepted notions concerning the physical basis of mental action, the first class must in some way be subsumed under the second. For it is clear that no consciousness can arise by mere *nonactivity* of a nerve organ, and therefore that the organs which *cease* to act in the case of the pains of restriction, and where pleasures of rest arise, cannot be the source of the pain and pleasure which arise in consciousness. Hence we may take it for granted that all pains and all pleasures will eventually be found to be statable in terms of *activity* of the nerve organs which are giving the consciousness at the moment of consideration.

The difference between pleasure and pain seems to be determined by some condition which goes with rest to the organs which are active in coincidence with pleasurable states. This leads us to surmise that pain and pleasure may be determined by the relation between the nutritive condition, which is affected by rest, and the condition of activity in the organs which are giving us the pleasant or painful consciousness; the pleasure being the accompaniment of the using up of surplus stored energy, and the pain arising when the stimulus calls for an overdraught of energy, if we may so speak. But these relations between activity and nutrition must hold for all of the nervous basis of our conscious life ; hence we must expect to find pleasure and pain to be general qualities, one of which must belong to each element of consciousness, and either of which, under the proper conditions, may belong to any element. The reader will remember that this is the conclusion to which we were brought by our consideration of the common-sense classification earlier in the chapter.

But my reader may protest, after having promised to touch so lightly upon psychology, Why have you led us through this long, distinctly psychological discussion ? Simply because I feel sure that this conclusion as to the general nature of pleasure and pain will make it very much easier for us to understand how it is possible to reach those summations and successions of pleasures which, as we have seen, determine our æsthetic field.

If pleasures are qualities attached to the
elements of our conscious life, then summations of those elements that are pleasurable
will make for us a total of pleasure which we
could not otherwise reach ; and summations
of the weaker pleasures we have seen to be
characteristic of æsthetic impressions. If
pleasure is so related to the elements of
our mental field, then also is it easy to conceive how, though the quality in them may
be evanescent, we may reach a relative permanency of pleasure, which we have claimed
to be essential to the production of the
æsthetic field, provided we shift from the
elements which give us pleasure at one
moment, and before this pleasure wanes, to
others which in their turn give us pleasure
effects.

Now let us turn back to an examination
of the general æsthetic theory reached in the
first chapter, and see how far it serves to explain the most prominent of æsthetic facts,

and how far it accords with the theoretical
views held by the masters of thought in the
past.

If it be true that the æsthetic field is determined by permanency of pleasure quality,
then the sort and kind of mental elements
that are thus pleasurable must determine the
nature of what we speak of as beautiful;
and, as people differ in individuality just so
far as they differ in the sort and kind of
elements which make up their mental life,
so we should be led to expect that the
nature of the conception of the beautiful
would differ as individualities differ. Clearly
this means that we ought to expect individual differences of judgment as to what
is beautiful; and, evidently, this is a fact
patent to all of us.

Differences of race, and differences of civilization in the same race, are determined by
differences in the common trend within the
mental lives of the individuals making up
the races compared. Thus we should expect

to find, what history most certainly shows
us, viz., a development of the notion of
beauty *pari passu* with the development of
racial life. The barbarian rejoices in decora-
tions by the use of brilliancy of colour and
strength of contrast. As his race increases
in culture, his mental life becomes more
subtle and delicate, and that which he calls
beautiful is correspondingly subtle and delicate in its nature.

So far as individual and racial development correspond, there is a similar change in
the notion of beauty in the individual as
he grows. The child of civilized parent-
age delights in much that the mature barbarian calls beautiful; when he has developed
towards youth, his beautiful objects are those
which appeal to the emotional life; but it is
not until later that he, with his full manhood, finds himself in sympathy with the
standards of beauty which are held by the
best-cultured men of his age.

The occupations of a race also, as they

determine mental fields, should thus be expected to influence the notion of the beautiful; and so do we find it. The chase, war, and actions determined by the coarser passions which are so prominent in the life of the barbarian make the subject-matter of his art, of what he calls beautiful. Examples of this we see in the art product of Egypt and Assyria, and in that of Greece. As the over-valuation of mere strength gives way, the subjects of art change to those which emphasize wider interests of life. The poets sing of nobler love; of moral action under difficulty. Our modern life, which has become introspective and thoughtful, brings with it a wider choice of subject treated with more refined intellectuality.

The forms of religious belief, so powerfully influential in all of life's products, as they change and develop, should also bring, as we find they do, alterations of the ideal forms of art. The Gods, represented by the Greek artist, give place to the Saints, repre-

sented in the works of the masters of Italy.
The Greek temple, designed to contain the
worshipped statue of a God, gives place to
the Gothic cathedral, with its spaces for the
masses within its walls.

If our principle be true, we should expect,
furthermore, to find theory influenced by
mental individuality in the theorist, and we
are able thus to account for the sensational
emphasis by a scientist like Grant Allen,
interested in neurology and sensational theory; for the emotional emphasis by the phi-
lanthropist Burke, and by the Frenchman
Guyau; for the intellectual emphasis by the
philosopher, as with Hegel, or with Schel-
ling; and for the spiritual emphasis by men
like Cousin and Ruskin.

Our principle also enables us to explain
the fact that opposed opinions are held by
men of the highest type under different conditions of thought: as an instance of this
opposition, we may note the Socratic emphasis of usefulness, which involves recognition

of an end; in opposition to the Kantian exclusion of recognized aim. The principle explains, also, the fact spoken of above, that men who are most susceptible to art in one direction may be dullards in another. The music-lover may take no interest in painting; the painter none in music or poetry; and this because their "faculties" are but partially and narrowly developed. It explains differences of view held by the same man at different times in his life; as an example of which we may refer to Matthew Arnold, who, in his essay on Emerson, says, "He is not *plain* and *concrete* enough; in other words, not *poet* enough"; yet in his essay on Maurice de Guérin we find him saying, "Poetry can awaken it" (*a full sense of things*) "in us, and to awaken it is one of the highest powers of poetry." The Arnolds in the two cases were different individualities, wrought into being by different forces, and expressing the different notions of beauty as regards a special art as felt by the two individuals at the different times.

The scientist's loss of delight in all that he had once called beautiful, as confessed by Charles Darwin, is also explicable when we consider that the very concentration which has given to the world his magnificent work, necessarily cut off from his mental life those associations which make possible the appreciation of pleasure of a relatively permanent sort, in connection with the objects which he used to call beautiful and which his most esteemed friends still called so. He surely had not lost all æsthetic sense, but he had truly lost the æsthetic field of his youth, and had paid the price for what he had attained in narrower fields.

In closing this chapter I would call attention to the corroboration of this view which is obtained when we consider that it enables us to understand the basis of the principal theories that have been presented to account for the nature of the beautiful.

Sensualistic explanations are evidently due

E

to an emphasis of the sensational inception of
æsthetic phenomena; to the forcible presentation of the fact that æsthetic *impression* is
usually largely sensational in character; the
exclusion of sensation by other thinkers being
accounted for by the fact that the so-called
"lower" sensations are so emphatically unpleasant in memory for those whose thought
is directed to ethical considerations. Emotional theories have their genesis in the every-
day, careless identification of pleasure-pain
states with emotional phenomena. Intellectual theories are naturally accounted for by
the fact that the mental life of deep thinkers
must, in its very nature, be largely made up
of rationalistic data, and that their pleasure-
fields must therefore necessarily tend to
the emphasis of the intellectual aspect if the
thinker considers the relations between the
elements of his æsthetic field: if he take another point of view and consider especially the
nature of the elements of his æsthetic life, he
is likely to lay stress upon the importance

of the imagination: while if he be impressed
with the importance of the reflective aspect,
he is likely to lay the basis of his doctrine
in contemplation.

Formalistic theories are based upon the
grasp of the fact that beauty must be determined by some quality which runs through
all of consciousness, and such a quality we
have seen pleasure to be. Absolutism and
Universalism, as we have already seen, find
their explanation in the relative permanency
of the æsthetic pleasure, and ethical and
spiritualistic theories are evidently due to
strong personal bias in the theorists who themselves can gain no revival pleasures in regions
that are not emphatically connected with what
is of ethical or spiritual import.

CHAPTER III.

The Art Instinct.

IN the first chapter we noted a distinction between the nature of the *impression* made upon the observer by a work of art or by a beautiful object in the world in which we live, and the nature of the *impulse* that leads to the production of an artistic result. The former subject we have been considering until this time; let us now turn our thought to the latter. This, the reader will note, involves an entire change of standpoint. No longer shall we consider Art as those do who are *impressed*, but as those must who *produce* æsthetic works; that is, we now undertake the study of æsthetics from the standpoint of the artist rather than from that of the observer.

The true artist is driven to his work by an overwhelming impulse. A man may, of course, deliberately determine upon an attempt to express himself æsthetically in some manner, to be an architect say, or a writer of verses, but this does not constitute him an artist, however much he may attain of skill in the profession he chooses. He shows himself a true artist when he appears *compelled* to the production of his art expression by an impulse that seems often to come from without himself, — to be a voice calling him, a muse inciting him.

Genius is distinctly instinctive. The true artist has a spark at least of the fire of the genius, and for that reason must depend upon his instincts, must be led by his impulses. Intellectual work and reasoned-out processes may be his tools, but they cannot take the place of the racial leadings which command his action in ways unknown and unexpected.

We all recognize that the genius is espe-

cially subject to hallucinations as the result
of the reflective absorption which precedes
his activities. He is liable to see visions
and to hear voices that appear to be real for
him, although none of his companions hears
or sees as he does. These hallucinations
are most marked in the case of the ethical
genius, — the prophet ; but that they are not
unknown to the artistic genius is apparent
from the legends of the muse that speaks to
the poet, and of the vision that appears to
the sculptor. It is said of Puvis de Cha-
vannes, who has given to the world the
magnificent decoration of the large hall in
the Sorbonne in Paris, that before he began
his work he spent days amidst the scaffold-
ings, merely contemplating the wall surface
he was to work upon ; and he tells his friends
that before he touched his brush he saw
clearly before him the decoration, exactly as
we see it on the wall to-day. This vision
was certainly not far from what a specialist
in nervous diseases would call an hallucina-

tion, and with such examples in our midst it is not surprising that the artists should still cling to the notion of inspiration from without themselves.

If we turn, however, from the poetical conception of this inspiration from without, and, taking a more scientific point of view, consider the subject of the impulse which guides the artist, it will seem worth while to endeavour to relate this "art impulse" to the other prominent impulses by which we are from time to time swayed.

To those who accept the probability of a developmental genesis in our race under the laws of control and survival, it will not seem surprising if our life-history show the gradual dawning and growth of certain co-ordinated instinctive reactions of the whole system, tending to the advantage and protection of the individual organism, and hence to the preservation of the race to which this individual belongs. We should be led to expect to find, still existing in ourselves, some general correlated systematic reactions such as were common amongst those of our progenitors, whose life was almost passive as related to its environment, in so far as these reactions still remain of positive value, or without disadvantage to us or to our race. We should expect, for instance, to experience (a) a wide instinctive reaction determined by the *approach* of an object, which has, in the past, been *advantageous* to the individual of the race, although it may not be known to the individual to be so; a condition of receptive expansiveness with reference to this approaching object. We should look (b) for a quite different, but equally wide, instinctive reaction arising upon the *approach* of an object which, in the past, has been *disadvantageous;* a condition of general contraction or shrinking, as it were. We should expect to find other corresponding mental phases differing in quality and elemental width, which would appear (c) upon the *departure* of the *advantageous* and (*d*) upon the *departure* of the *disadvantageous*. We should expect to find these reactions emphasized in our race, because it is clear that a race which did thus react immediately, in the manner and under the conditions named, would certainly have an advantage in the struggle for existence and would persist when other races without such capacity to react would be obliterated. Now if it be argued that there is a coincidence between nervous activities and mental changes, we should surely expect that, in connection with these more or less definitely co-ordinated instinctive activities, corresponding complex mental states would appear, and these for convenience we may call "instinct feelings."

We should therefore expect to find an "instinct feeling" —

A. arising upon the *approach* of the *advantageous;* another
B. appearing upon the *approach* of the *disadvantageous;* another
C. upon the *departure* of the *advantageous;* and still another
D. upon the *departure* of the *disadvantageous.*

Now, as a matter of fact, we do find certain complex mental states belonging to the class which we call the "emotions," that arise spontaneously and almost reflexly, and apart from any influence of our reason or will, and which correspond to the conditions above mentioned.

A. Joy, arising upon the approach of the advantageous.
B. Dread, arising upon the approach of the disadvantageous.
C. Sorrow, arising upon the departure of the advantageous.
D. Relief, arising upon the departure of the disadvantageous.

If we follow out the same argument in relation to our less passive life, we shall be led to a fuller comprehension of the nature of the emotions as a whole. I shall not ask my reader to enter into the details of a psychologic argument to prove my case here, but shall merely ask him to note that of the more varied emotions we find —

E. Love, which is connected with a tendency to *go out toward* an advantageous object, in receptive mood;

F. Fear, which is connected with a tendency to *flee
from* a disadvantageous object;

G. Anger, which is connected with a tendency to *act
to drive away* a disadvantageous object;

and we might also expect to find —

H. An emotion connected with a tendency to act in
such a way as would *attract* advantageous objects to us;

for otherwise there is evidently a lack of symmetry in our scheme.

But in fact we find no emotion H such as
seems necessary to complete this symmetry.
This fact may be accounted for by supposing
that this instinct *to-act-to-attract*, if it exist,
may be one which does not lead to any *immediate* reactive spasm, so to speak; and that
the reactionary effects, and the consciousness
corresponding thereto, would therefore be slow
to appear; and further, by supposing that
these acts brought about by this instinct may
be so varied that no fixed mental elements
would result from the instinctive reaction;
for with the Emotions A, B, C, D, E, F, and

G, just considered, this immediacy of reaction, and a certain stability of the elements involved in each successive reaction, must be supposed to determine the attention to, and the definiteness and fixity of, the "instinct feelings"; without this definiteness and fixity we could not expect them to have gained emotional *names*. For the attachment of names is a very late step in our racial life, whilst the instinctive reactions under consideration are determined by the experiences of untold generations of our ancestry before even the semblance of man's form had appeared.

That this supposition is not unreasonable appears upon considering the case of the well-recognized "imitation instincts," which must have corresponding "instinct feelings"; but if our argument be true, we should not expect to find emotional names attached to these latter, for the reason that the reactions involved are not immediate, nor of a definite fixed nature. As a matter of fact, we have no emotional state corresponding with the imitative activities, although the "imitation instinct" is recognized by all to be of fundamental value to us.

We have now reached a point of inquiry which seems, perhaps, far enough away from the subject of our chapter, but which I think will almost immediately show itself to be of importance and of very direct bearing upon the subject of our thought. What we are now led to ask is this: whether there be any impulses within us that lead us, blind as to the end in view, to undertake activities that will result in the attraction of advantageous objects to us.

If there be such impulses, we should expect to find in the first place tendencies to actions which would merely result in the attraction of attention to the individual; and such tendencies, recognized in marked degree amongst the higher animals, are clearly found in the human race in its barbaric state; nor can they be said to be totally lacking in the human species of higher types in our day. Prof. J. Mark Baldwin suggests that we call these activities the "self-exhibiting reactions."

Secondly, we should expect to find tendencies to produce objects or objective conditions which should attract by pleasing; and thirdly, we should look for tendencies to act to attract by the production of results useful to the one whose attraction is desirable.

The third class of tendencies is easily identifiable with those impulses to disinterested benevolence which are so prominent in modern life, and it may be noted here that neither the first nor this third class of instinctive tendencies result in immediate or definite reactions such as would lead us to expect the attachment of emotional names to their psychic counterparts.

What shall we say of the second class? Is there any widespread, instinctive tendency within us which, with no knowledge on our part of the end in view, still does work for results which shall please others, and which has no other *raison d'être* than this pleasure-giving; an instinctive tendency so slow in its reactionary development, and resulting in activities of so varied a nature, that no emotional name should be expected to attach to the reaction?

I think we have it in the blind instinct to produce art works; in what is usually called the "Art Impulse," but which I shall speak of generally in what follows as the "Art Instinct." The Art Instinct certainly is blind to any end in view except the expression of the ideals which are present to the artist's mind. It none the less does have the effect of producing objects which delight and which attract by pleasing; moreover, it certainly has in this a most valuable function, and apart from this no evident *raison d'être*. Furthermore, the impulse works itself out through slow and diverse processes which in their nature could not bring distinct and immediate reactions such as are necessary where emotional names are to become fixed.

Now I think my reader will see the drift of this long and perhaps difficult discussion, for it appears that our consideration of the subject from the artist's standpoint has brought us to the same conclusion that we reached, when in the first chapter we considered it from the standpoint of the observer; namely, that pleasure-getting and pleasure-giving are of the very essence of æsthetic phenomena, and that we should, therefore, treat the science of æsthetics fundamentally as a branch of the science of pleasure.

A discussion of this relation will appear in the later chapters. I wish now to consider some points of interest in connection with the art instinct as here conceived.

1. As far back as the time of the Greek Stoics, we find the art instinct spoken of as a development of the play instinct, and in later days Kant and Schiller and Herbert Spencer have emphasized this view. What, indeed, could be more natural than that such

an opinion should take hold of men, when we consider that it is only during our leisure moments, which are our play times, that we are able to look for the delights of beauty.

When one comes to consider play in its essence, however, he finds many difficulties connected with the doctrine that the art instincts are determined by the play instincts. It is, of course, well enough with Kant and Schiller to note and emphasize the bond between the two, viz., that both arise without definite known aims, with no evident human interests at stake; but when we look a little deeper we find that by play activities we mean those activities, usually thought of as "spontaneous," which, having no evident objective reference, have apparently no other function than the using up of accumulated energy; and upon a little further consideration it becomes clear that the simple "spontaneous" activities tending to the use of accumulated energy must have formed the starting-point of all developments of complex

F

activities, which were to subserve valuable ends in our more complicated life. The simple animal which was just able to meet the requirements of its environment would offer little or no field for developmental forces to work upon; but with the rise of spontaneous activity in some given direction, we have some chance of gain or loss to the individual which might determine survival or be the beginning of competition, and the basis of emphasis of special activities which would eventually turn out to be of value to the race. Without these simple "fortuitous" actions, so far as I can see, there would be no basis for the strengthening of special co-ordinations of activity by elimination or contest, survival or heredity.

I think, therefore, that we must hold that from this simple instinct to use accumulated energy, — this so-called "play instinct," — we must derive all those instinctive activities which we have considered in the first part of this chapter, e.g., love, anger, the imitation instinct, the instincts leading us to do what is known to be useful, and also, but with no *special* dependence, the impulse to do blindly what shall attract by pleasing, viz., the "art instinct." It is apparent, therefore, if this argument be sound, that it does not suffice in considering the genesis of the art instinct to look upon it as a development of play, but that some other explanation of its genesis is necessary, and such an explanation we have just been considering.

2. I wish to ask my reader to emphasize in his mind the fact that all the "instinct feelings" above described are altogether blind as to their end. We love and hate and fear spontaneously, and without any notion whatever that we are doing what nature calls us to do for the protection of the individual and race; and if the relationship exist between the art instinct and the emotions which I have sketched out, then we should find the art instinct impelling the man to his work without any apprecia-

tion whatever that he is really aiming to do what shall attract others to him. In other words, the art instinct under this view of ours is totally unselfish.

If this doctrine of ours taught that the artist works consciously for the pleasure he is to give, and which he sees will pay him in one coin or another, truly this would be false to the facts and would take the glory out of all art effort. But no such position is involved in the theory; for the true artist, in so far as he is an artist, has no end in view except the working out of his impulse to produce. So far as he learns to calculate and to mould his work in order that he may bring nearer a preconceived benefit to himself, so far is he led by other than the true art instinct; so far does he crush down his "inspiration," *i.e.*, the inborn tendency to produce æsthetic results, which, indeed, will bring pleasure to his admirers who are thus attracted to him, but this without any preconception of their value in this respect by the artist himself.

The art instinct is blind in its simplicity, with no end in view at all beyond the completion of its work. In proportion as ulterior determinate ends become fixed, the fire of artistic genius is dimmed, although the nobility of the man's work may perchance be heightened by the intrinsic nobility of his aim beyond the line of his art.

3. I would emphasize in the third place the fact, implied in the considerations above, that the instinct which leads to artistic work is a common heritage of man, as completely racial as are the more distinct "instinct feelings," *e.g.*, the emotions of joy and sorrow, love and anger and fear. We find men, indeed, of whom we say that they have never known sorrow, others who seem to be incapable of love, for instance; but very evidently we speak relatively in such cases; we do not for a moment lose sight of the fact that sorrow and love are emotions common to all of our race. And so it is with the art instinct: there are those who

upon a superficial view seem to be devoid of all appreciative or productive capacity in æsthetic lines, but for all that I think it must be granted that the æsthetic "faculty," if we may so speak, is a clearly defined *racial* possession, and is present to some small extent even in such a man as we have been describing.

The savage and the child equally tend to use up their surplus vigour in crude attempts to produce works such as, in their developed form, give us our best art products. Almost every adult feels some tendency to write verses, or to compose melodies, or to dabble with brush and palette, modelling-tool or draughtsmen's pencil. But, strangely, we find a notion prevalent amongst us that the existence of the art instinct in the young in any noticeable degree is a clear leading, and that the one who thus feels this instinct is especially "called" to devote his or her life to the production of art works; and yet who would think, because he discovered in his boy certain marked pugnacious tendencies, that the boy was "called" to the profession of a soldier, with a large chance that he would develop into a Napoleon?

We must remember that certain impulses that develop in childhood disappear entirely in after life, this probably being due to our individual growth by steps through forms that have belonged to our ancestors in the dim past. Capacities that appear to give promise in childhood may, therefore, be lost before the adult age. The presence of impulses in the young is, therefore, no sure guide as to the capacities they will develop in later years. Adult age, with its experience, must be reached before the man can become so especially skilful that he will stand apart from his fellows as one of talent; and this is true in all vocations of life.

It seems clear then that no one should feel that he is "called" to devote his life to æsthetic production, in the face of the knowledge that the life will be one of pri-

vation and pain, unless his artistic leading
is overwhelming in its power. Those of moderate talent can always find means of gaining a livelihood in the production directly or
indirectly of what is of use to their fellows.
Artistic work is essentially luxurious; it is
demanded *after* the needs of man are satisfied, and therefore only that which highly
attracts can be expected to "pay." The
man who has not great endowments as an
artist, although he may have acute percep-
tions and high standards, cannot hope to
succeed in making a living out of art work
of high quality, and if this view of ours be
correct, there is no reason whatever why he
should deem that he is called upon to devote
himself to the production of what must be
inferior æsthetic works, merely because he
feels this "art impulse" within him. Far
better were it for him to guide his energies
in directions which would lead to greater usefulness to the world at large, and in which
at the same time there would be less of pain

for himself and less of pain for the sympathetic public, who dislike to see the poor artist suffer as much as he dislikes the process himself. Were these facts given their full weight, many would hesitate, as they do not now, before undertaking art work as a vocation.

In bringing to a close our consideration from the artist's standpoint, we must touch to some extent upon the subject of our next chapter, in which we are to discuss the standpoint of the critic; for it is apparent that the artist must alternate between the attitude of the producer and that of the observer, and if he is to become an effective worker must be his own sternest critic.

Critical ability is connected with an analytic habit of mind, with a technical and theoretic knowledge, with a comprehension of the aims and ends of artistic endeavour, all of which are not uncommonly thought to be incompatible with the artistic temperament. The moments of production are indeed moments of guidance by instinct, as we have seen; but that this *abandon* to the guidance of the art instinct stands in no way opposed to the analytic life of thought is clear, when we consider that all artists do, to some degree, throw themselves into the frame of mind which is typical of scientific attainment in their study of technical methods, and in their consideration of the results they wish to reach. They must study to some extent; they must learn the rudiments, for instance, of perspective or of rhyme and metre, or of harmony and counterpoint; they must become skilled in analysis of their failures; so that any thorough-going statement of an opposition between the critical and productive attitudes suggests its own *reductio ad absurdum.*

The most that can be said is that the failure to combine in a high degree the two mental attitudes in one person is a matter of capacity, and that such capacity is not

often found. The more of a scientist and
critic the artist can become *without losing
the predominant habit of mind which leads
him to be guided by his art instinct*, the
greater will he be as an artist. The existence of such men as Goethe and Leonardo da
Vinci, who were esteemed as eminent scien-
tists, and who have made for themselves
enduring fame as artists, shows clearly that,
where capacity is great, results of importance
may be obtained by the same person in both
directions.

I think, therefore, that the development of
all that goes to make a man analytical and
scientific should be encouraged in the education of an artist: a man whose genius is
artistic will never be led away by scientific concentration. If a student be thus
led away, then surely it is evident that
his talent is scientific and not artistic; and
as surely the world will be a gainer in the
sequel. Artists of very mediocre talent
abound and multiply; it certainly would be

well if some of them were brought to see that they can do more effective service for the world and for art by devoting their energies to artistic investigation rather than to artistic production.

In my view, when the descendants of our race shall look back at the times in which we live, they will see some great æsthetic movement which we ourselves, perhaps, do not recognize, and will find some masters of æsthetic genius who will be seen to have had the force, as Shakespeare had in his day, to take hold of the main lines of the complex developments of our time, with all its new-born introspection and consciousness of aim, and who will appear, notwithstanding all this width of view, to have been willing to listen to the instinctive leadings within them which compel to noble art-expression. Artists they will be of noble mien, who can treat the burdensome complexities of our life as mere media of expression; and their work shall surely enlighten the path of all those who,

lost in the perplexity of this busy life, have
failed to grasp the fulness of its meaning.

There is a danger to the artist much more
subtle than that of loss of the art impulse
through serious study. I refer to the loss
of interest in the end to be attained, in consequence of concentration of thought upon
the means adopted to reach this end; and
it is evident that a knowledge of the science
and of the philosophy of art in its fullest
and widest sense will be a great aid in over-
coming this danger. That this danger is
real, and that much æsthetic endeavour fails
on this account to produce æsthetic result,
will, I think, appear upon the most cursory
view.

This danger, indeed, is one into which
workers in all fields tend to fall. All men
are liable to become absorbed by their interest
in the intricate machinery which they themselves have started in order to attain a certain end, and are thus led to forget the end

itself. In legislative life, the ordinary politician, even when he is not a self-seeker, fails to grasp more than the mere processes of enactment of the laws which are brought forward for consideration; in business life, the man is rare who is able to see beyond his immediate transactions; and the artist presents no exception to this rule.

The average musical virtuoso forgets his musical art entirely in his anxiety to perfect his technical skill. Orchestral leaders lose the very thought of the composer, take all "the soul" out of the music, in their attempts to produce accuracy in *tempo*, and perfection of special instrumentation. The painter is particularly liable to become absorbed in the search for some special element, the "values" perhaps, forgetful of composition or drawing or of other elements which are needful for the full perfection of his work. Architects are liable to forget all but the qualities of their drawings, of their compositions upon flat surfaces; oblivious of the fact that these drawings are merely instruments to the production of compositions *in the solid*. They draw in black and white with pen and pencil, and thus come to think in lines which can never be produced in their buildings, losing all sense of the proportions of the colour masses, which alone can make a building permanently beautiful.

The great artists, indeed, are those who do not lose sight of the fact that technique is but the tool by means of which they are enabled to express those special conceptions which come to them like inspirations, and which, when thus expressed, produce that permanency of pleasure which we call an effect of beauty.

I shall ask your attention for a moment, in closing, to what I consider the most important subject touched upon in this chapter, and perhaps in the whole book.

In all that has preceded this, we have been considering Æsthetics from an individ-

ualistic point of view. In the first chapter
we treated of the observer's standpoint, the
mental states of the *individual* as impressed.
In this chapter, in which, thus far, we have
been considering the artist's standpoint, our
thought also has been *individualistic;* has
dealt with the nature of the impulse that
guides the individual artist.

But the thought that has developed itself
enables us now to take a wider than individualistic position. Modern psychology, it
seems to me, has here a distinct message to
give to the students of the philosophy of
art, as this latter is a branch of the philosophy of life. The question which it raises
and answers relates to the function of the
art instinct in the development of our race.

The doctrine of development teaches us
that if an instinct is deep seated in the individual, it is almost certainly because it has
been of service to individuals as members of
the race. The art instinct is evidently very
deep seated within us, and has become elabo-

rated to a high degree; and it is exceedingly improbable that this would have occurred unless, in the following of this instinct, mankind had been subserving some valuable racial end.

In the scheme presented above, the reader will notice that so far as the question of function is concerned, the "self-exhibiting" reactions, the benevolent impulses, and the art instincts are all to be referred to the instinct to *act to attract*, spoken of under H above.

As we have no occasion here to discuss the "self-exhibiting reactions" nor the benevolent impulses, I shall speak only of the art instinct in what follows.

I think it is apparent, if my argument hold, that we now pass away from individualistic considerations. We find that the art instinct deals with the attraction of others to ourselves, unconsciously indeed, but none the less certainly for all that; in fact, it deals with the overthrow of isolation

G

and with the growth of sociality and sympathy. And, although I cannot agree with Guyau that the production of sympathy towards life is the end of artistic endeavour, I think we may surely say that the *function of art in the development of man is social consolidation.*[1]

Now, I beg to ask you whether this is not a noble and ennobling conception of Art? Is it not nobler than that individualistic view which for so long has taught us that as observers of æsthetic results the final end of our activities is to obtain personal delight; delight to be sure of a specially refined and so-called higher type, but personal delight for all that. We see in this view of ours a higher than individual significance in the emphasis of social sympathies.

[1] Since this was written has appeared E. Grosse's *Die Anfänge d. Kunst*, in which the author, approaching the subject from an entirely diverse standpoint, has been led to what is practically this same view. In the words of the reviewer in *Mind* (Nov. '94), he claims to show that the function of Art "is the strengthening and extension of social cohesion."

And taking our view from the artist's standpoint, is not this conception also a nobler one than the oft-repeated doctrine of individualistic values which in our day finds its best statement in the doctrine that the æsthetic end is "expression for expression's sake"? Is it not nobler, I ask, to conceive that the artist, while thus expressing his instinctive leadings, is at the same time the unconscious servant of Nature in her efforts towards social consolidation?

CHAPTER IV.

THE CRITIC'S STANDPOINT.

Concerning Æsthetic Standards.

In the chapter which has preceded this we have been considering Fine Art; that broad field of the still broader field of Æsthetics which is brought into being by the creative impulses of man; in other words, we there considered Æsthetics from the standpoint of the artist. In this chapter we are to turn again to the standpoint of the observer which we discussed in the first chapter, but with this difference, that then we considered the observer merely as impressed by beauty, while now we are to deal with him as one who judges; in other words, we are now to study æsthetic phenomena from the point of view of the critic.

84

Beyond the consideration of his impressions as an observer, the critic undertakes to become an arbiter as to the worth and the validity of standards. To the question of the nature of æsthetic standards, therefore, must we from the outset give our attention in this chapter.

We have seen that consideration from the standpoint of the observer, and also from that of the producer, of beauty, leads to the view that pleasure-getting and pleasure-giving are of fundamental moment to æsthetic theory; and in taking up this new point of view, our first thought must therefore be given to the relation which exists between pleasure and the nature of æsthetic standards.

We have seen that from the field of æsthetic impression we are able to exclude no pleasure, whatever be its character, unless it bring with it *at the time* an overbalance of pain. Any pleasure that can in any way be brought into connection with other pleasures to the formation of a pleasurable complex state, so that the several elements form parts of a whole, or so that one follows the others in an associative train, by this fact becomes part of the field of æsthetic *impression*.

But with the field of æsthetic judgment the case is quite different. The field of æsthetic impression will include as part and parcel of its totality many impressions that are pleasant in themselves, but that are not pleasant in revival, and which on this very account will be excluded from the field of æsthetic judgment which is determined by the pleasant nature of remembrances.

The ephemeral nature of pleasure, and the variation that this implies in the character of the revivals from which we are able to gain pleasure would lead us naturally to look for an

(A) *Individual Standard of the Moment.*

Favourable judgment under standards of this type would be determined by the fact that the mental phases of the special moment of thought under consideration are composed of pleasant revivals. This individual standard of the moment is that to which we refer when we make off-hand judgments in æsthetic matters. In its nature it must be exceedingly variable, for it is changed by each variation in our surroundings, by each alteration of associative train, by every difference in our physical condition.

Taking up, first, the influence of surroundings, we may note that patriotic songs, like "Marching through Georgia," or "Hail Columbia," which appeal to us at a military tournament, would seem crude at Bayreuth; and that *Parsifal*, which overwhelms one with its æsthetic effects, under proper conditions, could not be appreciated at all at a county fair.

Differences of associative train determine our "moods," and we easily recognize the difficulty one has who, being full of joy and gladness, attempts to catch the full beauty

of an Israel's "Alone in the World," or of
one of Millet's peasant studies; and equally
well are we acquainted with the failure in
the sad and sorrowing of the capacity to
appreciate wit and humour. And so of differences of physical condition: the invalid
finds beauty in gentle, soothing music; but
it is the vigorous man who craves the fire
of Liszt and the surging, tumultuous stream
of Wagner's creations.

But this individual standard of the moment
is quickly recognized to be unreliable, and we
learn to appeal to a higher standard, which
is still individual, but which relates to a less
variable field, viz., to

(B) *The Relatively Stable Individual Standard.*

Judgment under this standard is determined
by the fact that the fields of momentary revivals change not infrequently from pleasure
to pain, or at least lose their hedonic quality
in indifference, if held for any length of time
in consideration; and we are therefore led to

judge as to what is beautiful by those fields
that retain their pleasantness after the enthusiasms of the moment are gone. These
fields are the basis of the judgments that we
make after reflection, and they determine our
personal tastes. From them are cast out all
that reflection shows us to be painful in any
well-recognized case, or indifferent in all but
unusual cases. To these fields we look in the
careful comparison that goes with the analysis of a work of art, while, as we have seen,
the æsthetic fields *of the moment* are the basis
of our casual every-day judgments.

But it must be noted that we are still dealing with fields that are only relatively permanent; with standards that are liable to
change from year to year, and, to a lesser
degree, from day to day; for it is clear that
as these standards are determined by the individual mental constitution of the man, they
must change, as do the man's mental fields,
with growth and development and alteration
of environment. The æsthetic standards of

our youth are remembered with laughter in middle age. My little girl exclaims with delight, at sight of a beautiful sweeping wave: "Oh, how beautiful! It reminds me of the most delicious of desserts." On the other hand, in the sombre days of life's decline the enthusiasms of one's prime seem extravagance; those of the child sheer madness.

The effects of habit, too, are here most marked. Habit changes the current of our thinking, and altering, therefore, the fields that are recalled with pleasure, changes our standards. The doctor, as I have noted above, learns to call a fine preparation of cancerous tissue beautiful. The average artistic Parisian learns to think his modified classical Renaissance architecture to be all beautiful, finds in the Romanesque masterpieces nothing but barbarity, and utterly despises everything English.

It is because habit is so powerful an agent in the formations of our standards, that width of view and of education is so important in

art matters. If we individuals constantly surround ourselves with objects which the race
of cultivated men as a whole has declared un-
lovely, we shall nevertheless all too soon learn
to forget their enormities, and actually may
come to feel a sense of loss when we do not
find them with us. We are, to a large extent, responsible for, as we are to some extent
the makers of, our own standards in Æsthetics as well as in Ethics. It is because of this
formation of bad standards through miseduca-
tion, that I think the cultivated public ought
to take a deep interest not now taken in the
education of architects; for in the nature of
the case the architect's work is often not
ephemeral; it cannot nearly as easily as the
work of other artists be removed or obliterated from thought by inattention, when it
is found distasteful; and thus it must remain,
if it be bad, a permanent evil influence, tending to lower the standards of those who are
to come after us.

As we have said above, we are evidently

still dealing with standards that are only relatively permanent, that are constantly liable to change. Few of us ever realize this variability, this shifting nature of individual taste; but as soon as we do realize it we refuse to be satisfied; we ask for something more certain and stable; we do not care so much what a person's individual judgment is, as what it ought to be. To reach the æsthetic "ought" of the hedonist, of him who believes in this dependence of beauty upon so variable a thing as pleasure, is not the simplest thing in the world for man, as he is ordinarily constituted. The average man never reaches it. He is unwittingly the most ardent of absolutists. His own personal taste he believes to be a reflection, as it were, of a certain fixed absolute, and if others differ from him, it is, in his view, because they are thoughtless, or are led by other than æsthetic influences, or are not sufficiently cultivated to appreciate what is good. He is content to deal always entirely with subjective standards; and when he would have something less variable than the individual taste of those who surround him, he canonizes his own taste, and makes that the standard.

But it is evident that this individualistic standard of personal taste can have no philosophic validity. If we are logical hedonists, when we feel the need of some criterion more stable than our own tastes, we must turn from the consideration of our own special, limited, individual, æsthetic field to one which is as distinctly objective as any absolutist could demand ; viz., — to

(C) *The Æsthetic Field of the highly Cultivated Man as we conceive him.*

This is the field which every philosophic critic must acknowledge, apart from his own individual taste, if he is to treat æsthetic matters with any breadth. The individual peculiarities of his own field, whilst they must remain none the less valid for himself, must be treated as individual rather than general ;

and his criticism must be determined by reference to the broader than individual field which contains all that is common to those for whom he speaks.

This standard, my reader will perceive, is still really changeable and unstable, but *relatively* speaking, it is unchangeable and stable, for its variations are determined by processes of wide reach and slow development. It must vary with width of experience, of education, of refinement. It will change as a person limits his notions of life and of the universe, or as his views become broader and more sympathetic. It will alter with variation of his conception as to what is worthy in the world surrounding him, and as to the sincerity and value of other people's beliefs; and in the end it will be found to be largely determined by his ethical conceptions. This fact is expressed by Wundt when he says, "Effectiveness of higher æsthetic representations depends always upon the arousal of moral or religious ideas." The same general conviction is expressed by Taine, who, although no hedonist, would have us measure a work of art by its importance and beneficience, that is, by its power to develop and preserve the individual, and the group in which the individual is comprehended. Similarly, Fechner would have us make our own final standard of æsthetic valuation dependent upon our conception of what, on the whole, has the best outcome for the well-being of mankind, for time and eternity.

The relative stability of this standard gives it objective force as a real existing Ideal. Professor Royce has lately emphasized the view that our notions of reality in the world about us are, to a great extent, dependent upon the possibility of comparison by individuals of effects upon themselves *and others*, and by the perception of agreement in the experiences involved; in other words, dependent upon social recognitions, or, as he puts it, "it is social community that is the true *differentia* of our external world." With this

view in mind it becomes clear that the standards that we are now discussing must become
objective in a sense that allies them closely
to the realities of the external world. For
in the conception of these standards we are
taking account of the agreements in the
experience of those whose judgment we believe to be most worthy of confidence, and
are endeavouring to co-ordinate our own
experience with these agreements.

In emphasizing the value of the recognition of other standards, however, we must
not overlook the fact that individuality of
field is none the less important, for upon it
is dependent

(D) *The Ideal Æsthetic Field.*

This ideal field, from our standpoint, must
be a variable one, differing for each individual; no Absolute as usually conceived; no
fixed objective Platonic ideal, towards which
we weakly strain; but the field which in
some direction differs from the normal field,

and in this direction the individual feels that
the world *ought* to agree with him. Each
one of us, however prosaic, has some sort of
an ideal field of this kind; non-agreement
with it in others looks like æsthetic error.
So firmly rooted is this belief in one's own
ideal that intolerance is proverbial among
artists and connoisseurs; intolerance which
is often amusing to one who looks at the
subject from a student's standpoint. Once
in a while an individual Ideal, when expressed, enlightens the world of art, and
then we have the artistic genius; he is the
prophet who shows to others an ideal field
which they at once recognize as effective
for themselves, although but for him it would
have been unknown to them. To express
his own ideal must the artist work. He
must indeed produce effective results in the
field of presentative æsthetic enjoyment, but
if his work is to be of importance, it must
go beyond the momentary effect; it must
compel recognition as part and parcel of the

H

stable field of pleasurable revival (B), and must not stand opposed to the objective standard which is given by recognition of the value of the opinion of others, whose cultivation entitles them to speak with authority (C); if, however, the work of an artist is to be recognized as that of a master, it must express an ideal (D) which the common mortal, however highly cultivated, does not and can not reach of himself, but which he will recognize, when it is reached by another, as an enlightenment of his own duller conceptions.

Now I wish to ask my readers to note the nobility of this standard of relativity.

The conception of an absolute standard, which we have discarded, the notion of a fixed Universal Beauty, which the artist strives to conceive and to represent, has in itself great æsthetic value, altogether apart from its philosophic value; it attracts us by the relief it offers from the distracting oppositions of individualism, and by the fact that it arouses within us that certain sense of sublimity (itself an æsthetic state), which attaches to all things that are dimly felt to exist, and yet are but indefinitely realized; to all that which on account of inscrutableness invites worship.

But if we lose something in adopting the standards of relativity, I think we are on the whole gainers. For it is apparent that our view tells us that the sense of beauty is never to be lost to us. If an absolute fixed beauty existed and were once attained, if its principles were once known so that they could be applied to all of life, then surely with this, as with all else of human attainment, its commonplaceness would involve loss of interest for us, and in the end our race would be deprived of one of the best gifts and of one of the strongest of incentives to noble action; that is the capacity to appreciate and the tendency to search for new expressions of beauty.

But the doctrine here defended enables us

to look forward to an ever new and ever higher conception of beauty, arising as man develops towards nobility and perfection. As these standards are determined by subjective states, as they differ with human attainment and enlightenment, so evidently must they be determined by our character; as that develops towards higher worth, so will our estimate of Ideal Beauty continue to develop, ever disclosing to our view new glories, and bringing to us new enthusiasms; so will beauty continue to enlighten our path and alleviate the burdens of life, and still remain as an incentive to nobler living and higher thinking.

Before we turn from this subject of standards I will again remind my reader of a point touched upon in the preceding chapter. Hedonism in Æsthetics is for many difficult to accept, because it seems to them to savour of what is ordinarily called Epicureanism. If it were true that æstheticism merely teaches selfish pleasure-getting, if the artist were led to work merely to give pleasure that he might thus gain advantage to himself, then surely we could not complain if our ethical masters were to renew ascetic attacks upon all emphasis of æsthetic culture. But as we have already seen, there is no warrant under our theory for any such view. The artist follows, blindly as to the end in view, the voice of a leader, the guidance of an impulse, and the one who judges rightly of beauty is as far removed from egoistic influence as is possible under any of the circumstances of life. The very forms under which the higher art necessarily presents itself, force self-centredness to give place to sympathetic width of view; the cramping limitations of egoism break down in the æsthetic atmosphere.

I have spoken above of the development of standards, of the fact that our standards do and must change with our growth and development, and I wish to call attention to this point once more because it has an important bearing upon æsthetic pedagogy. If objects appear beautiful to us as they are able to produce in us a sense of living, permanent pleasure in revival, then it is evidently impossible that we should perceive beauty in an object unless it does produce these permanent pleasures. The youth who has never felt the strong bitterness of human suffering, cannot be expected to appreciate the beauties of Shakespeare's *King Lear*, nor can the child who knows not yet the fulness of mature human love be expected to enjoy Wagner's *Tristan and Isolde* in its entirety. Each person's perception of beauty must be determined by his capacities of associative thought. It is useless to give meat to babes, as valueless, indeed, as to feed vigorous men from the breast. We too often expect youth, or those of low mental endowment, to appreciate beauties which can be grasped only by men of capacity, who have given their years to the acquirements which make appreciation possible. It is absurd to expect average young children to gain anything but *ennui* and a sense of distress and dislike from concerts of symphonic complexities, and all such attempts are in my opinion foreordained to failure.

It is vain also to hope to revolutionize the standards of taste of the people living in the " slums " by giving to them exhibitions of paintings of such merit as can only be appreciated by mature men of the fullest development. There may be a lesson of sympathy in such action by the so-called "upper classes," but there is little æsthetic hope in it; of that I am convinced.

It is altogether futile to attempt to force æsthetic standards upon others; what we should aim at is the development within the young and the ignorant of the capacities and mental activities which will not only enable them to appreciate art work of high value, but will lead them spontaneously to go out in search for it. To attempt to force our own standards upon them, either produces disgust or despair, most seriously opposed to the development of a refined æsthetic judgment; or else, and all too often, an insincere pretence of appreciation, which is evidently immoral in effect.

The most fruitful lesson that is taught by this doctrine of relativity is one of liberality, of tolerance of other's standards, of humility as to our own. As we have seen, the æsthetic field of childhood is not that of the youth, nor that of the youth the same as that of the man of mature years. Differences of cultivation and of point of view necessarily involve differences of standard, and must be constantly taken into consideration. As we see the advance we make from childhood's standards, as we hope to gain still more perfect ones with our further culture, so must we be willing to recognize the validity for others of their standards which are not ours, and study them to see whether they may not have in them elements by which our own can be improved.

We must not expect that others will agree
with us in our revival-pleasure-getting, except on the broadest lines. The failure to
recognize this fact is often a serious loss.
The belief that beauty is something absolute,
which he has mastered, brings to many
a man fulness of *ennui*, and leads many another to a hopeless cynicism, when he finds
that what he has learned to consider pre-
eminently valuable begins to pall upon him.
Such is the position which too many a critical
mind reaches, and which would be avoided
could the critic but look beyond the standard
which he himself has set, and take cognizance
of the manner in which his own æsthetic
field alters and develops as he grows in constitution of mind and life.

Now let us consider a few points of direct
application to the critic.

There is a feeling current to no small
extent that there exists an opposition between the critical attitude and that of the
artistic producer; an opposition which some-

times appears in fierce denunciation of the
critic by the artist, and which again voices
itself in objection to the intellectual, critical
treatment of æsthetic subjects in general, on
the ground that such treatment, if encouraged
in a man or race, is likely to curtail in the
man or race æsthetic production of high
grade.

The study of art history, it must be confessed, has tended to substantiate this notion
of the inverse relation of art production to
intellectual consideration of æsthetic matters;
for as it shows ages which are unproductive
of art work of high value; it seems also to
show that the age of non-production has
often been one of devotion to pure critical
formalism.

It seems to me, on the whole, that it might
better be claimed that the studious age has
been the parent of the productive one; but,
at all events, the facts are in all probability
accounted for, not by any lack of critical
spirit during the ages of great art outcome,

but by the emphasis of critical work which the absence of notable art production brings into prominence.

So much for the grounds for this opinion. That the opposition is superficial is clear however, for as we have already seen there is no opposition between the mental attitude of the student and of the producer, the former is surely the helper of the latter; and further we must remember, as we have already noted, that the critic is no more than the student observer, who deals with analysis and with the determination of the validity of standards, and furthermore that the artist must upon occasion take the place of an observer, and will do better work in so far as he becomes his own most serious critic. It is evident, therefore, that there is no fundamental opposition between artist and critic.

But it is true that in practice the critic far too often assumes an attitude of hostility. A man may indeed devote his life to superficial carping, without having sympathy with, or without ever knowing, the artist's aims or methods ; but surely this is not worthy of the name of criticism. It is this superficiality that irritates the artist, and which is not for a moment to be condoned. To become a worthy critic, one must be not only a deep student of the philosophy of art, but must make himself conversant with the artist's technical methods and his personal aims. If the artist have limited views and aims, his spirit and his work cannot be properly appreciated by one who is expecting to find views and aims other than the artist's, and equally limited in other directions. And here we strike the greatest difficulty in the mental constitution of our critics. They are seldom broad enough or accomplished enough. They have learned to know well some little corner in the wide field of æsthetic endeavour, and they judge all else in the field by the standards thus reached. Perhaps it is the lover of Wagner who fails to see beauty in music that deals with clearer melody and more formal counterpoint. Perhaps it is one who feels deeply the study of "values" in painting and forgets "composition," and subject, and all else in the picture before him, judging it by comparing its "*values*" with those of the master whom he worships. Perhaps it is a lover of Milton who refuses to see strength in the work of another whose style is more free, and whose conceptions are more mystical. The critic, and the artist so far as he is his own acute critic, must, it is true, consider first the delights of immediate impression, but he should never forget that the vivid elements, which dazzle for a moment, are the ones of which we most surely tire, and that fuller, more permanent, and more fundamental delights must grow upon us as this vividness disappears, if the æsthetic work is to remain a permanent acquisition to Art.

The emphasis in the critic's mind, of a limited phase of æsthetic endeavour, is thus liable to produce within him narrowness of view which vitiates his judgment. This is a special danger attaching to the purist's standpoint. Habit, in the æsthetic life, as elsewhere, easily comes to dominate us. A man may, by the emphasis of certain formal characteristics of art products, learn to disdain a work which fails to come up to his standard in these particulars, whilst he altogether overlooks graces and strength in other than these formal directions. Perhaps the greatest danger the critic has to guard against is that of the artificial creation within himself of petty standards which, when shocked, give a sense of ugliness sufficiently predominant to prevent the appreciation of wider beauties which should determine his mature judgment. Width of education, width of view, but especially unbounded sympathy, — these are the qualities which the critic should encourage within himself as a safeguard against the pitfalls we have thus brought into view.

I cannot close this brief discussion of the critic's standpoint without saying a word concerning the responsibilities which go with the critical attitude; and this is said not only to the professional critic, but to each and all of my readers; for all of us at times assume the part of the critic in the eyes of some of our companions. It is so easy, as I have already said, for a critic, whose word is heeded, to make and unmake standards of art for others, to make and unmake æsthetic objects. On the one hand, excessive praise of some work of moderate merit will result in the attachment of importance to that work for all time in the eyes of those who trust our judgment; and on the other hand, it is equally true that derision or blame given to a work of power will continue to lower its value with those who trust to us, long after they have discovered for themselves that the art work has value for them. Let us all then, when we act as critics, look well to it that we use the influence which we wield for æsthetic good and not for æsthetic evil.

CHAPTER V.

Negative Æsthetic Principles.

IN the chapters which have preceded this we have seen that Æsthetics may with propriety be considered as a branch of Hedonics; as being dependent directly upon pleasure laws, and indirectly, therefore, upon the laws of pain. Hence the title of this chapter: the word "algedonic" (ἄλγος, *pain*; ἡδονή, *pleasure*) being used to cover the whole ground of pain and pleasure.

In Chapter IV. we have considered our subject from the standpoint of the critic, and have learned to appreciate the importance of width of view, and of liberality of judgment concerning others' standards: but our ideal standard has been fixed by the considerations of the first and third chapters. The end to which the æsthetic producer works is the creation of objects which shall be beautiful for the highest type of man; or, to use more technical language, the creation of a full, and relatively permanent pleasure-field of revival in those who are the representatives of our highest ideal of manhood, and in whom the trend of development is towards the noblest forms which human thought is capable of showing.

We are now to ask what help we may obtain in the practical search after beauty, and in our judgments concerning others' like efforts, from our study of the nature of pleasure which we see to be so all-important for both worker and critic-observer. If our theoretical study be worth anything, it should be possible for us to deduce certain general laws of æsthetic practice from a consideration of the conditions upon which pleasure-getting depends. It should also be

I

possible, in some cases at least, to trace the practical application of the principles discovered, in the empirical rules adopted by æsthetic workers, and perhaps finally to find the psychological bases upon which have been built the æsthetic theories which we find it necessary to reject, although they be taught by high authorities.

It will be well, I think, to restate succinctly the algedonic-æsthetic theory which we are to develop in what follows.

The Beautiful is that in nature, or in the activities or productions of man, which produces effects in us that in retrospect remain permanently pleasant. I have spoken of this so fully above that I do not need to enlarge upon it here.

The Ugly, on the other hand, is that which produces effects that remain permanently painful when viewed in retrospect. For instance, a most disagreeable, painful, and altogether ugly set of impressions may be obtained in connection with the action of

saving a man from suffocation in some nau-
seous chamber. But in the revival of the
scene, which occurs when we judge of its
æsthetic quality, the pain has gone out of
the presentation, and the nobility of the act,
and all that this nobility implies, sweeps
away the ugliness, and makes the act one
of commanding beauty.

If a natural object, or the production of
the artist, is to be effective as an æsthetic
object, it must bring not only pleasure by
its mere presentation, but, more than that,
it must result in the production of pleasant
revivals, that will coalesce with that field
of pleasurable revival which in reflection we
call our æsthetic field. The artist must
employ all possible means leading to the
attainment of immediate pleasures so far as
these are compatible with the production of
pleasures in revival. He may add much in
the way of mere presentative pleasure which
perhaps may not bring us pleasurable effect
in revival; and all such added pleasure in

presentation is a gain to the work as art, provided it neither bring pain in revival, nor swamp with resulting indifference the revivals that are pleasant. He may even go further, and add elements which give decided active painfulness in the direct presentation produced by the examination of the art work, provided the result in revival be on this account made more permanently pleasurable. He may use pains of restriction, in either presentation or revival, in moderation, if they are treated as indices of fulness of pleasure to be reached when the restrictions are removed.

Even in the mere examination of art works, we must take account of revival fields; for we lose much if we restrict our attention either to the detail, or to the mere totality before us. Unless we allow the play of revivals to have full sway, our best enjoyment is gone.

While pleasures in primary presentation, therefore, are important, the pleasures of revival are of pre-eminent moment in æsthetic consideration.

Our task here amounts simply to a consideration of the means to be adopted to produce a pleasure-field of relative permanency.

All will agree, I think, upon two points which I wish to emphasize at this moment.

First, that pain is incompatible with pleasure, or, in other words, that *with a given element of consciousness*, the conditions that involve pain must be absent if the conditions that involve pleasure are present. Second, that there is a field of non-pleasure, which is also not painful. This is the field of so-called *indifference*, which, although theoretically narrow, is practically wide in extent, because often the variations from the moment of indifference towards pain or pleasure are so slight as to escape notice.

Now, it is evident that both of these fields of non-pleasure, both that of pain-getting and that of indifference, are to be avoided before

we can reach pleasure with any given set of
mental elements. The field of pain must be
entirely eliminated, unless its occurrence is
useful for pleasure-production to follow; that
of indifference must be suppressed so far as
is necessary in order to avoid the overwhelming of the pleasurable elements by those
which do not interest us.

Negative Æsthetic Principles.

It is evident from what I have just said
that we may treat as the first principle of
æsthetics

The Exclusion of Pain; the Elimination of the Ugly.

We all realize that there are practically
two great classes of pains. First, the pains
produced by repression of activities; and,
second, the pains produced by excess of
active functioning.

I have elsewhere shown, I think, that in
all probability the first class must be referred

to the second; active functioning apparently being necessary to pain of any kind. As a matter of practical experience, however, we find two means by which we may *produce* pain, viz., by the repression of activities and by the hypernormal stimulation of activities. This fact, which doubtless has prevented the earlier recognition of the common basis of all pains, makes the current distinction between the two classes of pain perfectly legitimate for us who are here concerned with methods of pain *production.* We may, therefore, properly divide our first principle into two subsidiary ones, — (A), the avoidance of repressive pains, and (B), the prevention of pains of excessive functioning.

(A) *The Avoidance of Repressive Pains.*

Repressive pains occur when a mental element, a thought, an object, which would have appeared in consciousness if the conditions remained normal, for one reason or another fails to so appear. This may· happen (1st) where the mental element habitually arises in a rhythmical manner in answer to certain stimuli, provided these stimuli fail to appear at the usual time. Examples of this form of repressive pain are found in connection with our quasi-vegetative activities, of which breathing and its resultants throughout the system, and digestive processes are examples; the pains of suffocation coming with the holding of one's breath and the pains of hunger and thirst arising from abstinence from food and drink are due to such repressions. These pains are to be avoided, of course, if we are to obtain a pleasure-field, but as no one who desired to produce an æsthetic work would think of giving it such form that its appreciation would be dependent, for example, upon the holding of one's breath, or upon the existence of the mental states which we experience when we hunger or thirst, there is no reason why we should enlarge upon this point. These special repressive pains are induced only by the production of abnormal conditions, and in a search for means towards pleasure production, such as Æsthetics is held to involve, we should expect to find them *naturally* avoided, as we do.

There is another kind of repressive pain, however, which is of much more importance. I refer to those pains (2d) that appear if mental elements arise which normally would bring out, would act as stimulants to the production of, other mental elements, these latter mental elements in fact failing to appear. We are all familiar with such cases. At a certain time of the day some voice or sound calls us to dinner, or the gong in a lecture-room tells us that our hour of effort has ceased and that some time of pleasant relaxing conversation has come. If some business necessity prevent our going to dinner, or if the persistency of our lecturer prevent immediate relaxation of attention, we all know the uneasiness that follows. All cravings and desires fall under this heading; they are all painful states caused by failures of fruition in directions in which our mental life would naturally have developed.

Well, these pains also are to be avoided if we are to reach pleasure in connection with the elements involved, and the principle here enunciated would seem to teach that the artist must, in general, avoid the stimulation of cravings which cannot be satisfied, the production of desires which are impossible of fulfilment, the suggestion of lines of thought which cannot be completed.

It is not apparent, however, at the first glance, that any such canon of practice is recognized by artists or critics. Indeed, on the contrary, many works of art which we all agree to be of the highest order of excellence, are distinctly felt to produce these longings of a dull and indefinite sort. But when we consider the matter closely, we see why no such rule is acknowledged; for it is evident that these pains will be admissible, in a way, provided the observer's thought is thereby turned in new directions of pleasure-getting.

It will be admitted, I think, that it cannot be the proper aim of an artist to induce *strong* cravings, *intense* desires, *fierce* passion. It cannot be forgotten that as long ago as the days of the Greek supremacy, the power of artistic work was felt to lie largely in its capacity to *dispel* the passions, to *purify* the objective through the ideal. Those art works which evidently induce lesser unsatisfiable longings, as of love and pity, or which bring desire for what is unattained or at the moment unattainable, gain their power, it would seem, not through the pain so much as by the flow of sympathetic activity which is produced, or by the impulses which are awakened, or by the revival of old-time thoughts which in their wide reaches are ever delightful. It is in reflection that we are most powerfully affected by these works of art. As we, in revival, view the mental state which was induced by their study, we feel the sympathetic delights which give them worth, or we see that they brought to us impulses that we hold to be of highest ethical value, and which it must always give us the deepest satisfaction to feel that we have possessed. With the bitterest pains of repression, we contemplate the portrait of one whom we have loved but lost; and yet, with the pains, are aroused so many trains of memory which tell of joy, that we return again and again to the contemplation. We would not give up the pains, for without them were impossible the renewal of other deep satisfactions.

But there is another point to be brought forward here to account for the permissibility of the guarded use of repression in æsthetic work of high quality. A careful study of algedonic theory will show us that the existence of repressive pains is an indication that the mental element which fails would appear pleasurably if it appeared at all. If, then, the pains of craving can finally be replaced by the pleasures of satisfaction of the craving, it is apparent that the pains of repression, within limits, may be encouraged by art workers, for the very sake of the after effects of pleasure to be obtained. The pains of repressed activity indicate, as I have elsewhere argued, an organic condition of full preparedness, so that if action supervenes it will bring the highest degree of pleasure that can be induced by the organ's activity. These repression pains may, therefore, be taken as an index of pleasure capacity, and we may expect them to be used by the artist, because thereby he will gain certainty that the pleasure limits have been attained, and that a full pleasure will accompany the action which is to follow the repressal.

Dependent as such transformations from pain to pleasure are upon the succession of psychic states, we should look for notable practical exemplifications of them in arts that deal especially with phenomena of succession, *i.e.*, in music and in literature. In music, we have example in the delayed resolution of a chord which is allowable even to the point of painfulness. In literary work, we have example in those every-day complications of plot which delay the consummation longed for, and finally reached. Schiller, speaking of tragedy, tells us that " the highest degree of moral pleasure cannot make itself felt except in conflict. It follows, hence, that the highest degree of pleasure must always be accompanied by pain." The principle is one of wide import in all branches of Æsthetics, and here I think we have its basis; for, as we have seen, organic rest is a most important condition of pleasure production. How are we to know that we have gained full capacity for organic functioning unless we wait on the wide systemic pain which comes after the absorption of energy has reached its maximum?

We have here also the psychologic basis of many a metaphysical theory of the relation of the Ugly to the Beautiful, and of the value of the presentation of the Ugly as an element in the Beautiful, as instances of which we may note Schlegel's dictum that the principle of modern art can only be found if beauty and the characteristic ugly be indissolubly connected ; and Rosenkranz's statement that the artistic genius finds the highest triumph of his art where he represents the ugly objectified, and beauty all-powerful through triumph over evil. Ethical notions and metaphysical conceptions here lead us away from psychology proper, however, and this we must avoid.

The most important of all repressive pains for our consideration, however, are those which arise where certain mental elements often appear in definite relations of succession, the usual order of this appearance remaining unfulfilled. Evidently this class of repressive pains will not be of infrequent occurrence in our experience, for they depend upon combinations in varied orders which are easily alterable, and which, on the other hand, are grasped with such difficulty that we in our weakness cannot for a moment hope to be able to avoid the repressive conflicts they engender. We should, therefore, expect to find some recognition of occurrence of these pains and some general attempt at their avoidance in æsthetic theory and practice. It is these pains which make up the very usual form of ugliness which is determined by the combinational effect of many disappointments of expectancy, each painful, in too small a degree, indeed, to be emphatically presented, but for all that, helping to make up an aggregate of undefinable but emphatic disagreeableness.

Let me quote from Schiller again. In one of his interesting and suggestive studies he tells us that "beauty can tolerate nothing abrupt nor violent." In other words, if an object is to appear beautiful to us it must not bring to us shocks of any important kind. The lines, the forms, the colours, the sounds, which we find in nature, resultant as they are from the influence of cosmic forces in conjunction with growth, bring to us certain arrangements of stimuli, which, though complex beyond our power of analysis, must mould our

nervous system into preparation for the recep-
tion of stimuli in corresponding orders and
arrangements, and this in psychological terms
means the production of a tendency to the
rise of certain special mental states in special
orders and relations to one another.

If, then, nature presents to us, as she does,
with relative infrequency, objects which bring
stimuli in relations contrary to those in accord
with which our systems have been moulded,
we should expect to note just such shocks of
repressive pain as nature's monsters produce
in us, quite apart from the active pains (of
aversion or fear, for example) which they
may superinduce.

In our productive work, it clearly would
be indicative of an intelligence far above that
which we possess if we did not find ourselves
too often bringing about combinations of
stimuli which violate the order that nature
has impressed upon us.[1]

[1] The reader will understand from what I have said
elsewhere how it is possible for a person to gain "an ac-

K

Illustrations here crowd upon us. All of nature's lines are affected by the power of gravitation. It seems clear to me that the relative grace of the suspension-bridge as generally constructed and of the cantilever truss-bridge is principally determined by the fact that the catenary curve in the former case presents to us nature's pendent form, while the strutted extensions of the cantilever bring to us other lines than those in accord with which she has educated us. As one's eye follows the lines of the cantilever truss, natural organic combinations bring preparation for action in certain directions. But the stimuli to these activities fail when the abrupt and rigid lines break off in directions which nature has never given us; the shocks of repressive pain that result produce that sense of discomfort which we express by calling the work ugly.

quired taste " (an acquired pleasure capacity) which will in the end make these unnatural forms not unpleasant and even enjoyable through appreciation of other values than those which are natural.

One who stands by the brink of Niagara, with its ever-flowing lesson in the curves of gravity, cannot help feeling strongly that the lines of the suspension-bridges are in satisfactory harmony with the scene, but that the cantilever bridge makes a blot upon the landscape almost as unfortunate as the rigid forms of the factories built upon the river's bank. It seems to me that the beauty of the rocket's flight is also largely determined by the submission of its movements to the laws of gravity.

The same principle may be recognized in visible forms quite apart from their contour lines. The relations of the parts in the human figure vary in an indefinite number of small ways, but any marked disproportion of parts at once gives us the shock of ugliness. It is comparatively seldom that nature brings these positive shocks, although often the men and women we meet show little of positive beauty. In the creative representations of man, however, nothing is easier than to produce such misemphasis of relations, and such unnaturalness that ugliness in whole or in part is induced.

Even more delicate are the relations of colours. "Is it not strange," a lover of flowers once said to me, "that nature does not give ugly combinations of flowers when it is so easy for us to combine them in an unsatisfactory manner?" This commonplace observation teaches the doctrine here discussed. Nature, through the influence of the prehistoric past, has been our teacher, and to nature's colourings we must go to learn what combinations to make use of in our work of rearrangement, and, if we may so speak, of re-creation. If we break away too far from her guidance, we have our punishment in the shock of perceived ugliness.

When we turn to sound relations we recognize the disagreeableness of sudden changes from the habitual movements in music; if, for example, some unskilled performer strikes an incorrect note in a known progression, or if the development of a harmony be broken by an erroneous chord.

Here we find ourselves prepared to step away from nature's teachings to the more complex regions of mental effort, which depend upon habits artificially formed, if we may so speak, in the process of development. The principle will be recognized as the same, however, whether the pain be caused by breaks away from habitual combinations, produced by nature's wider and racial, or by more narrow and individual, influences.

The related forms which our race through many generations of experience has learned to feel to be most satisfactory, cannot be lightly disturbed without producing painful distraction. This we all feel in those lines on which practice enables us to judge with discrimination. The mere novice objects to a Gothic window in what purports to be a " classic " building. The more highly educated student at once revolts against a façade of Corinthian detail massed in Doric proportions or with Ionic intercolumniation; and this is due to the fact that he has learned by observation how these special parts have been best related by the long study of successive generations in the past. The work of one who disregards this racial experience brings to the expert a shock, which for him makes æsthetic delight impossible.

As I have noted in the preceding chapter, the same principle holds with the purist's judgment in all art work. The critical student is all too apt to create within himself, artificially, petty standards which when shocked give a sense of ugliness sufficiently predominant to prevent him from appreciating the wider beauties in the work before him.

It seems to me that we have shown clearly that in repressive pain we have the main source of ugliness, and we are led to the conclusion that it is most important to avoid pains of repression as preliminary to the production of beauty.

Now I wish to turn to the consideration of certain negative laws of great importance, which depend upon the principles just discussed. These laws in a number of cases we shall find to have been already recognized, but erroneously, I think, as positive teachings of the contraries of those principles which should rightly be emphasized.

We are all too ready to fall into logical pitfalls connected with incorrect use of complementary opposites. Experience tells us that we must avoid *not x* if we are to produce a beautiful object; *x*, therefore, is fixed upon as the basis of beauty.

It is clear, after what has just been said, that were we to start out from a theoretical basis we should be inclined to hold that our safest course of procedure would be to *imitate nature*, sifting out her especial beauties, or recombining her elements, so that relatively permanent pleasure would result for us; for thus we most easily avoid shocks which go so far to produce ugliness. In fact, it appears that this is what the great mass of artists in almost all lines of effort do to-day, and what they always have done; and it was this observation, so far as we can judge, that led many authorities to look upon *imitation* as so important a principle of art. It is apparent, however, that imitation is a means to an end merely, and that it is not possible to make it fundamental for all art. It appears to me that it is a principle of importance rather negatively than positively. It guides us in the direction in which beauty will be found, and far outside of which it cannot be found; but that it gives us a positive basis for the production of æsthetic result, I think untrue, as must be evident to any one who does not exclude architecture from the realm of æsthetics.

Our true principle here is not *imitate nature*, but is this: *avoid radical departures from nature*, for such departures must surely bring to us the shocks which produce ugliness.

Other examples of the same logically illicit

procedure, and of the consequent misnaming of principles, are not wanting, some of which deserve mention.

Freedom from shocks implies *avoidance of inharmonious relations;* and perhaps it is not surprising that the observation of this should have raised *harmony* to the dignity of a first principle, notwithstanding that the most cursory examination must show any unprejudiced person that we are fairly enveloped in a world of harmonies, which give us no æsthetic result at all.

So, again, *uselessness, unfitness, abnormal departure from type,* must be eliminated if painful shocks are to be avoided; and without such avoidance no effect of beauty can be obtained. From this source, it seems to me, have arisen the doctrines of the relation to the æsthetic of *usefulness,* of the importance of *fitness,* of the necessity of *conformity to type.*

It is true, indeed, that no egregious departures from our typical standards, no marked unfitness in the object presented, nor any emphases of qualities which are hurtfully useless, are possible without producing this pain. But it is as far as possible from the truth to hold that departures from normal types within limits are non-æsthetic. On the contrary, it is just such departures that add piquancy to much which we admire.

It is equally misleading to argue that the non-useful cannot be beautiful, or, as is more often the case, to overestimate the importance of the recognition of the useful in given æsthetic fields. So far as the useful can be considered as a *positive* principle, it is covered by the principle of the summation of associative pleasures, which we shall presently consider. Perceived usefulness has often been made an essential point in architecture. Usefulness truly becomes more important in this than in other arts ; not, however, *per se*, but through the strong emphasis of the painfulness of each useless feature which exists to the detriment of the whole. It is not improbable that the superior pleasure obtained from ancient works of architecture is in some degree due to the fact that they have lost their capacity to shock through opposition to the immediate needs. The limitations of human capacity are so great that shocks of this kind are forced upon us in every newly constructed building, made to serve some distinct purpose, however great be the skill of the designer. To be sure, each use may add to the complex pleasures of activities associated with the use, and these associative pleasures will be cut off in disappointment pains, when the lack of this usefulness is noticed; but here again it is the non-æsthetic effect of the non-useful, and not the æsthetic effect of the useful, which tells, and which forms the basis of the so-called principle.

Mr. Spencer also holds, as Emerson held before him, that the useful tends to become beautiful; but so far as this is true, it is not because of the usefulness *per se*. It seems much more naturally explicable as one of the phenomena of habit; for, as is well known in a great class of cases, activities which have become habitual gain for themselves pleasure capacities, either directly or associatively. Another point made by Mr. Spencer serves to illustrate our contention. Style, he thinks, depends upon the reduction of friction to a minimum in the chosen vehicle. But surely this is merely a negative principle,—a condition preliminary to the use of those satisfactory forms which mark a good style in whatever material the artist works.

If the reader will allow me another illustration of my contention from the works of Mr. Spencer, I think one may be found in that treatment of gracefulness, adopted by him, which makes its delights dependent upon adaptation to ends. Grace without this adaptation is, of course, unattainable, but that is merely a negative description of its field. If Spencer's position were correct, we should be compelled to grant the quality of gracefulness to a perfectly ordered machine, and to shut out most important elements which have no relation to fitness whatever; *e.g.*, the delight which we gain from those flowing curves which our retentiveness pictures for us in and through movements, the sympathetic pleasures which Schiller has described as dependent upon "beauty of form under the influence of freedom," without appearance of the strife and conflict which willed actions entail; and we should be forced to leave out of account many other elements of associative worth.

Turning in another direction, it appears that the doctrine which makes the expression of truth an essential principle of art has a similar negative basis. Untruth, in all the arts, is a source of great dissatisfaction; but this merely gives us the negative principle *avoid untruth!* it gives no ground whatever for the teaching of realism that the preeminent aim of the artist should be the expression of truth.

With architectural forms, better education

teaches the observer the natural action of constructional elements, and brings about uneasiness unless there is evidence of their consideration in the building-up of the masses: it is natural, therefore, that we find the principle of "truth" constantly reiterated as an especially valuable dictum of architectural æsthetics; but for all that, the real principle is the "avoidance of untruth."

Here we may mention the demand for repose in architecture and in the plastic arts in general as another negative principle, founded in this case upon our appreciation of nature's law of gravity. Repose *per se* will not bring us æsthetic joy; but without it, in the cases cited, beauty cannot be reached. The building must be felt as stable, the human figure must "stand upon its feet," or be poised in a position it could occupy in nature without continued strain; but these conditions may well be fulfilled without result of æsthetic moment.

Let me illustrate this general point once again. Growth is a law of nature. Everywhere around us we see forms which are of marked type indeed, but which present evidences of developing change in non-essentials. Art works which present evidence of such growth gain great power through sympathetic harmony with nature and with our own developing selves. The evidence of this verisimilitude of life, perhaps unanalyzed and not definitely recognized, probably adds much, for example, to the attractiveness of the Gothic cathedral, and emphasizes the poetry of the structures of Northern Italy. Musical forms also are especially fertile in producing these living effects. Music which is mechanically produced can never give full satisfaction.

But surely it is not in evidence that the expression of growth or of life can be held to be the fundamental in æsthetics, as some would have us believe. At the most, the effects produced by the representation of these qualities can be but an adjunct to other means of impression. For certain people, however, who become accustomed to look for them, they may be demanded when absent, for the purpose of eliminating a painful need, and may thus become for them necessary to æsthetic result. This, however, shows no proof that they are the essential to æsthetic effect in general.

The unities which the Greeks made so essential in the development of the drama gain their force negatively, for without such unities distractions must be felt from the line of thought in which the poet would guide his hearer. That this is true is shown by the lessened demand felt for the unities of time and place in the drama of modern times; for, through historical study, the grasp of eras has become as common to-day as that of individual lives; and, with us, movements from place to place, widely separated, are matters of usual occurrence.

Let us now turn from the consideration of the avoidance of repressive pains to the second division of our principle as relating to pain; that is to

(B) *The Avoidance of Pains of Excessive Functioning.*

So important is this avoidance that works of art are in all cases developed on lines in which excesses may be shunned with little difficulty. So soon as the work of the artist begins to tire us we must be able to turn away from its consideration. The stimulus given must directly or indirectly be under our control, so that we may grasp the opportunity for enjoyment when, and only when, we are in the mood for the special pleasures involved. There is no more certain manner of destroying our appreciation of any special art work — that is, of making it non-æsthetic for us — than by compelling attention to it when we are weary in the direction of its peculiar stimulus.

L

Here we have a lesson for the teacher of the young.

As we have seen, a certain class of repressive pains are *naturally* avoided, and with pains·of hypernormal activity nature aids us also very materially, for we tend automatically to prevent excess by the shifting of attention. Concentration and permanence of attention upon one subject are certain to become speedily painful; indeed, because of the reflex effort towards avoidance, they are, strictly speaking, impossible under normal conditions, except by means of a cultivated habit, and then only through the artifice of "looking around the subject," so to speak; of allowing the various details to be viewed in the mental focus without letting go the primal theme which is held in associative trains. As avoidance of pains of this type is comparatively easy and almost automatic, it is natural to find that theoretic consideration has dealt less with them than with those repressive pains, not naturally avoided, which

are the result of unexpectedly encountered pitfalls, only to be missed by much prevision.
That excesses must be shunned is taken for
granted. This is the principle involved in
the oft-repeated Aristotelian emphasis of the
necessity of adopting a mean between ex-
tremes.

Taking the realm of pain as a whole,
we may state our principle as that of "the
avoidance of the ugly," as we have done at
the opening of this section. It is by this
process that the artist gains the broad background which he must win before he can
realize his ideal of beauty. His results must
give many a pleasurable element, and, as we
shall presently see, some special points of intense interest, but he cannot hope to make
the wide mental field which his work arouses
altogether pleasurable; the most that he can
hope for is that it shall be devoid of elements
of possible painfulness.

It is in this direction that the *science*

of æsthetics will always produce its most valuable effects. Its work for art must always be to a great extent negative. If it teach us what have been the principles which advancing art has shown, it is to enable the artist of our time to avoid carelessly putting out effort in directions opposed to these principles which without being recognized have guided the artist in the past. If it show us some necessary relation of the phenomena with which the artist deals, it is that he may learn not to waste effort in vain endeavour to treat his subjects in a manner contrary to these necessities. The anatomist teaches the artist what the relations of bone and muscle and tendon are in the physical framework, so that with help from this source of knowledge he may create his ideal form without the dissatisfactions which go with the presentation of false anatomical relations. The mathematician teaches perspective, that the artist may *naturally* avoid what would be disturbing anti-perspective errors, into which he might fall in his enthusiastic concentration upon the expression of his ideal.

Science in truth must always follow where creative genius leads, in whatever direction it is developed; but for all that, science has a most valuable function to perform in relation to art.

The importance of this elimination of the ugly which scientific æsthetics enables us to make will be acknowledged when it is considered that special interest in the work of art as at first presented may very easily blind one to many elements in the work. If these latter are displeasing, they will become effective to cast the work out of the realm of æsthetics as soon as the intenser interests pall upon us.

All men naturally follow out the general maxim here discussed, and it is to a great extent through accumulation of such eliminations of ugliness that our standards of artistic excellence have been reached. On

general lines the bad has been sifted out
or allowed to fall into the background as
time has passed, and the noble and beautiful has been left unaltered because it has
been felt to be too satisfactory to require
change.

Most of us are wont thoughtlessly to look
back at the architectural forms of Greece as
the creation of her golden age. But it is
clear to the student that those splendid
achievements embody the thought of many
generations, and even of diverse races, rather
than that of a special era of a few generations' continuance. Generation after generation had felt the same needs in their worship,
had built and rebuilt temples as their inferior
materials and workmanship, or the more
actively destructive forces of nature, compelled. Each new work had made it possible
to eliminate some form which had been displeasing in the last effort, to alter some unsatisfactory surface, to change some deficient
shadow depth. In the final results we see

the record of untold endeavour towards the attainment of beauty, mainly successful because time and experiment have effected the complete elimination of the ugly. The growth of Gothic forms, of which we have better knowledge, tells the same story of experiment and partial failure; of renewed effort with avoidance of the elements which made the last work unsatisfactory; until we reach the glory of the best Gothic, less perfect than the Greek indeed, as it expressed the demand of a race impelled by less unity of feeling, and as its growth was forced within the relatively short period of perhaps a thousand years.

Too great difficulty of applying eliminative experiment may indeed be looked upon as a bar to development. The Egyptians, to whom the expression of permanence seems to have given the greatest satisfaction, built in such ponderous material and so durably that change of form for them was a matter of far greater difficulty than with the Greeks, whose materials were less permanent and much more easily worked. This difference doubtless accounts largely for the fact that we find Greece in a relatively short time gaining possession of such a flower of architectural art as had failed to spring from the stem that had grown for long ages in the climes of Northern Africa. It is no little comfort for us in these restless times to see how few of our buildings are constructed to endure in the future. If, with our changing needs, we have little ability to develop an architectural art, at least our descendants will not fear to sweep the greater part of our work from the face of the earth.

The possibility of making these eliminations is curtailed by everything which tends to emphasize fixity. The rules of the schools, valuable as aids to the student, always carry with them the danger of repression of "the elimination of ugliness." Note how the rules of counterpoint stood in opposition to the development of music; how the establishment of the "orders" in Roman architecture struck the life out of the Greek architectural development; how the dictionary thwarts the natural development of euphony in language.

We see the main principle enunciated again in our own times and in our own homes. Comparatively few of us can fill our homes with objects that remain for us, or for our friends, permanently beautiful. We may be able to have a gem here or there, but that is all. Still we may avoid "shocks," and in that avoidance lies much of the power of a cultivated mind in architect or householder. To this is surely due the beauty that *grows into* the homes of those whose culture is handed down with the building that passes from one generation of refined people to another. The inhabitants learn to brush away the "shocks." The inharmonious lines and forms are covered; the harmonious lines and forms are retained; gradually and unwittingly they mould their surroundings to relations which do not clash ; and in such an environment the smallest beauties tell.

In looking over other art fields, where the medium of expression has been in less permanent material, it is difficult to realize how much work has been done which has been cast aside because of inferior worth, has been allowed to deteriorate, and thus has been lost. It were much more difficult did we not realize that our race is in the main not far removed from those that time has swept away before us, and did we not see this process of production and elimination going on around us to-day. Practically a vast proportion of the pictures preserved in the great galleries of Europe have been eliminated from the æsthetic. We go to these vast treasuries to study a few pieces of work ; all the others are passed by as if they did not exist. If we could reproduce the sudden barbaric intrusions of the past, it is easy to see that the few precious gems which time has taught us to value supremely would be hurried off to places of

safety, while all else might readily be eliminated by vandal destruction or neglect.

It is evident, of course, that the attainment
of an unpainful background in itself will not
suffice to bring about æsthetic result. Not
only must the artist avoid pain in indifference,
but before gaining the pleasure-field he must
move beyond this field of indifference. This
brings us to our second division, which, however, we may pass over lightly, for indifference, as we all recognize, may be avoided only
in the directions of pain and pleasure. Pain,
as we have just seen, is also to be avoided by
the artist. The attainment of pleasure is,
therefore, the only means by which we can
step away from indifference in a direction
that will be not unæsthetic, and we are therefore at once brought to the consideration of
the positive field of æsthetics, to which we
turn in the next chapter.

CHAPTER VI.

ALGEDONIC ÆSTHETICS. II.

Positive Æsthetic Principles.

IN the chapter which has preceded this we have considered the preliminary steps that must be taken by the artist who aims towards the attainment of beauty, and now we must try to discover the positive laws which lead to effectiveness in æsthetic endeavour, or, in the words of our æsthetic theory, must look for the means and methods that are necessary to *the production of a pleasure-field which shall be relatively permanent.* It will be convenient in our discussion to treat separately (1st) the production of pleasure itself, before considering (2d) the means adopted in the attempt to reach *permanency* of pleasure-field.

156

I.

First, then, as to the production of pleasure. We have already seen that pains are practically produced in two ways, and so it is also with our pleasures; they, too, are practically produced in two ways, and are consequently naturally divided into two great classes. We have, first, the pleasures which arise with rest after strain, with relief from pain; and, second, those that arise in connection with active functioning, in connection with vigorous, healthful exercise of our faculties.

The pleasures of rest after labour, or relief from pain, as we have already seen, although really to be considered as a subclass under the pleasures of activity, are in practice separable from them, because they are reached in practice by distinct methods. Unquestionably, use is made of them in the arts that deal with phenomena of succession. It is no slight pleasure, for instance, that we obtain in music by the introduction of a calm, restful movement following upon a train of intense and vigorous passages calling for our active attention. But, on the whole, these pleasures do not form an element of marked importance in æsthetic work, and especially for the reason that they are so dependent upon the existence of, and are usually so inseparably connected with, anterior pains. We may pass on, therefore, without further examination in this direction, to the consideration of the pleasures connected with the vigorous exercise of our faculties.

In our second chapter we saw that the relation of rest to pleasure seems to teach us that pleasure is due to a use of surplus stored force which has been accumulated in the organ which is called into activity in coincidence with the element of consciousness that is pleasant.

Now there are several means by which this use of surplus energy may be brought about, and if the hedonic æsthetic theory be true,

the study of these means should lead us to
the recognition of certain principles of æsthetics which depend solely upon these means
adopted in the production of pleasure. These
several methods of pleasure production evidently may be used at one and the same time,
but it is desirable for us here to treat them
in isolation.

First, we should expect that a mental element which has often arisen in consciousness,
but which has for some time been absent,
would bring pleasure when it does appear;
and this because its organic coincident will be
rested and vigorous and because there will
therefore result a use of surplus energy when
it does act. Examples of this will easily
occur to the reader; the taste of sugar, to
which we have become accustomed, but of
which we for a time have been deprived
under medical advice; the appearance of the
face of a friend who has ordinarily been a
daily companion, but who has been away from
us for some unusual time.

The principle of æsthetics here presented is the principle of *contrast*. Contrast in any region of mental effect involves the presence of mental elements that have not been in consciousness in the late past. It involves the action of organs that have not been active during the immediately preceding moments. Gradations in sense effect or in thought transitions are mental movements, which imply the *gradual* coming into action of the organs which are successively the centres of activity. Contrast eliminates all gradations; it involves the action of organs, which through mere rest have become well prepared for activity, and which, therefore, produce pleasurable activity when stimulated.

That contrast is an important means to the attainment of æsthetic effect is recognized by all; indeed, it is not infrequently overvalued, *e.g.*, by Mr. Herbert Spencer, who calls it an *essential* requisite to all beauty. But our theory would teach that contrasts are not æsthetic essentials, because pleasure can be

reached without contrast by mere increase
of vividness, as we shall presently see. For
all that, it must be granted that the principle is of the widest application, and a
most available one for the guidance of the
artist. It must be noted, however, that
very strong contrasts cannot be used without
the greatest caution; they give powerful effects, but effects that are rapidly exhaustive,
and, therefore, they must in general be
avoided. To this we refer later under the
consideration of permanency.

Now let us consider a second means of
pleasure production closely allied to the one
just studied. When a mental element which
is often occurring in certain connections is
inhibited, as they say technically, i.e., is prevented in some manner from arising in consciousness, then upon its reappearance we shall
have it pleasurably presented because, by the
very process of the inhibition of its organ's
activity, surplus energy has been stored
up in this latter and this surplus force is

M

called out when the organ again acts. We have already discussed this form of pleasure production in the last chapter, where we showed why and to what extent it is permissible to encourage repressive pains in æsthetic effects, for these repressive pains are due to the inhibitions we now speak of. We there saw that these pains may be allowed, because they serve as an index of the fact that we have reached the limit of highest pleasure-getting in connection with the mental element which will appear when the repression disappears; with this disappearance of repression the mental state which has been repressed recurs with full pleasure. As we then said, "Dependent as such transformations from pain to pleasure are upon the succession of psychic states, we should look for notable practical exemplifications of them in arts that deal especially with phenomena of succession, *i.e.*, in music and in literature. In music we have example in the delayed resolution of a chord which is allowable even to the point of painfulness. In literary work we have example in those everyday complications of plot which delay the consummation longed for, and finally reached."

The principle under discussion becomes important in another direction. If there arise, by suggestion from the expressions of another, trains of thought which are normally connected with other secondary trains, but if by skilful management the arousal of these secondary trains be prevented, then we have a condition of artificial inhibition which will result in pleasure-getting whenever the secondary trains are allowed to appear.

Such, it seems to me, is the process in the delicate play of wit.

In what is usually called the "ludicrous" we also use this means of pleasure production, although much of the effect in such cases is dependent upon sudden transitions, in the lines of ordinary association, from mental processes which involve effort to more habitual processes where the same energy will produce greater effects; *i.e.*, hypernormal stimulation, which we shall presently discuss more fully.

Of course, we can but touch upon this subject here; but I think it can be shown that while other sources of pleasure-getting are made use of in various ways, together with the action above described, this latter is the characteristic movement. in what is usually called the "ludicrous"; and it seems to me that it serves well to harmonize the oppositions of the many thinkers who have attempted analysis of this mental state. Those cases of the ludicrous which seem to involve little except surprise are explicable on the ground that the surprise involves attention and expectation of important outcome: when the unimportance of the object or action is perceived, the relaxation of attention results in the same powerful overflow into the channels of ordinary activity. The easy and marked "step from the sublime to the ludicrous" is also thus explicable, as is also the enjoyment we receive when we see a dignified person suddenly take up the actions characteristic of purposeless childhood, — as when a man's hat is suddenly carried away by the wind.

It cannot be claimed that all such transitions, from mental processes involving effort to others where the same energy will produce greater effect, as are above described are ludicrous, for thought trains of discovery and invention are not infrequently of this nature, and to them surely the word "ludicrous" cannot be applied. Introspection seems to tell me, however, that the mental conditions in the two cases are very closely allied. We have a tendency under such circumstances to laugh, or at least to smile, under the pleasurable excitement; and we occasionally speak of the resultant as a "happy thought." I am inclined to think that the difference, at first one of degree rather than of kind, has become marked because the more emphatic and fuller state produced in us by what we term the "ludicrous" has become indissolubly connected with what Kant describes as "the sudden transformation of a tense expectation into nothing."

And now to return to the subject of wit proper. The wit, properly speaking, plays around his subject, avoiding the more usual outcome of the train of his thought, but leading that of his hearer close to this normal resultant, until, when it may be supposed that all the organs connected with the normal outcome are fully prepared for action, he turns the thought train in the direction which is effective for pleasure. The stimulation of the well-nourished organs, which the previous inhibition had thus involved, is followed by the burst of pleasure-giving activity which irradiates the system, and expands its surplus energy in the pleasurable exercise of laughter. These exercises of laughter are pleasurable in such cases because they, too, involve the action of rested organs. The more serious aspect of things, from which we turn to the perception of the ludicrous, involves partial if not total quiescence in all those organs which are notably active when we laugh.

Puns and plays upon words give delight in the same way, as do also the delicious verbal misunderstandings of children. My little daughter once asked what was meant by Anglo-Saxon, and having been told that the word indicated a mixed race descended from Angles and Saxons, she answered, "Well, I suppose I shall understand it some day; I have not yet come to Saxons in my geometry, but I have studied about angles." She obtained no delight in the saying. For the listeners, however, the sound *angle* had brought about readiness for activity in the organs of many trains of thought connected with geometrical forms; but the added term Saxon had kept the attention completely in other directions; when the thought was turned to the geometrical trains, however, by the child's naive remark, the well-prepared organs responded with pleasurable consciousness.

It must ever be remembered, however, that

the wit and he who deals with the ludicrous tread on dangerous ground. The clown perchance may not cause laughter, but may disappoint us so painfully that irritation results. Apart from the danger that the witticism may cut too deep, there is the danger that the repressed activity may force itself upon the attention of the hearer before it is designed to appear. In this case the course of thought which is intended to lead up to the latter becomes obstructive to the known resultant, and the consequence will be a sense of weariness; this is exemplified, for instance, in the "flatness" of old jokes. Further, there is the danger that the play around the subject may develop trains of so much interest that the change of thought will produce a shock powerful and painful enough to overbalance the pleasure led up to. We all realize how dangerous it is to treat lightly subjects which may be of sacred interest to others.

A third means of pleasure attainment is found in mere vividness of presentation after normal absence from consciousness, the surplus stored force being brought into use simply by unusually powerful activity of normally efficient organs.

Vividness of impression is a well-recognized means of producing æsthetic result in its cruder form. Barbaric art shows this distinctly, and the art of the masses, even in our day, makes use of the same means. Vivid colouring and contrasts, startling forms and combinations, vivacious rhythms, loudness of sound as in martial music ; all these are common tools for the popular artist. But we here tread on ground dangerous to permanency ; for hypernormal activity, as we have seen, is the basis of pain as well as of pleasure, and pleasure which is determined by this alone must be of a very ephemeral character. The surplus stored force is soon used up, and if the unusually vigorous activity continues pain must result. So it happens that in the higher art this crude means of producing æsthetic effect is not prominent.

In a more delicate form, however, we do find it of service to higher art in the stimulation by varied means of the same activities at the same time, thus producing the vividness which goes with hypernormal stimulation. The principle here involved is that of "harmony" or the "unification of the manifold," which is widely recognized as of the highest importance in æsthetics. Harmony implies the existence of some common quality in two diverse mental objects.

If this principle were not over-emphasized by high authorities, it would be unnecessary perhaps to call attention to the fact that, although wide in its bearings, it cannot be universal as the cause of all beauty. Fechner, who certainly makes as much of the "unity of the manifold" as is legitimate, acknowledges this (see p. 42 of his *Vorschule*, where he mentions several instances to which it is not possible to give this explanation). We are evidently surrounded by appearances of unity in manifoldness that do not impress us with

sufficient pleasure to give the objects producing them the quality of beauty, the slight
pleasure which they give being overwhelmed.
On the other hand, many beautiful objects appeal to us in which we can trace no distinct
element of this unification. Æsthetic effect,
indeed, as we shall see, implies more than
the vague gentle pleasure which the unity
of the manifold, as it usually appears, can
produce.

The principle of duplication of stimulations,
of which the unity of the manifold is a special instance, is, none the less, a most important one for æsthetics. As Mr. Sully says:
"To wake up to a resemblance between two
things hitherto kept apart in the mind is
always an agreeable experience"; and again,
"The feeling of satisfaction which accompa-
nies the full reinstatement of the idea or idea-
complex arises from the identification of this
with the partially developed representation
that has been present throughout the process." Throughout the whole field of the

"higher" æsthetics, — *i.e.*, of that which deals with the delights arising from the more delicate play of mood and thought, — this means of pleasure production is most important.

On the whole, I think it must be granted that the mass of æsthetic pleasures is reached by slightly vivid presentations in varied directions, but, as it has just been noted, this very vividness leads to loss of pleasure. How then shall pleasure permanency be reached, is our natural query, and this furnishes the subject-matter of our second division.

II.

We have already noted three points; (1st) that vividness of impression is an important source of pleasure-getting, but (2d) that the avoidance of continuity of vivid presentation of any one set of elements is a necessity if pain is to be avoided. But it is clear (3d) that the shifting to avoid continuity brings about those cónditions where absence of a mental element from consciousness for an unusual time, suffices to make it pleasurable when it appears. If, then, a permanent pleasure-field is to be reached, a vivid "focus," if we may be allowed to use this term, is important in our field of consciousness, but this focus must shift from element to element, and this shifting itself involves new means of pleasure-getting. In general, therefore, we may say that the conditions of pleasure *permanence* are the shifting of a focus in consciousness over a wide pleasure-field. Let us consider each of these divisions more fully in reverse order.

Width of Field. — Pleasure in any one direction being essentially ephemeral, the only means by which we are able to ensure permanence of pleasure is by having open before us wide opportunities to change the content of our thought. As we have already seen, it is first of all essential that the fulness of our complex mental states should be non-

painful; it then becomes important to see
that many elements of the complex are
capable of developing pleasure. This is
important not only because we are thus
enabled to shift the focus of attention with
little risk of painfulness, but especially because
a multiplicity of simultaneous effects thus
becomes possible. Lotze, as he views his
consciousness, tells us that the æsthetic effect
" is notably (but not exclusively) bound to
simultaneousness and multiplicity of impression." It is thus that the artist groups
together as large a number of means of
pleasurable stimulation as he can combine
without conflict. He endeavours to use at the
same time arts of ear and sight, and those
which depict more directly the activities of
men. The difficulty of such wide combination, however, is very great, and he more often
deals with narrower fields; but always does he
use every device which may draw into the field
of suggestion all associative factors which are
not inharmonious, and which may add some-

thing to the pleasures given. He does not disdain any element, however likely to pall, if he is able to leave our thought free to turn elsewhere as soon as the pleasurable effect is gone. The suggestion of sense pleasures he uses, but avoids the actual sense stimulus under conditions that may lead to excess or bring painful results in revival. He aims to bring into play the imagination which carries one on from height to height in pleasure-giving flight. It is this direction of effort which leads Lessing to call for an incompletion of detail in the artist's work, that the imagination may have room in which to work its expansive effects. We look thus for a fulness of non-fulfilment of exact detail; for an avoidance of strictness of realism — for type portrayal. The artist, moreover, aims to stir up those vague regions of pyschic life, the elements of which we can scarcely grasp,— the regions usually termed "emotional." He produces in his observer an æsthetic horizon which Guyau has interpreted, wrongly I think,

as the essential characteristic of æsthetic
pleasure; that "irradiation" which seems to
have a centre in some sense impression, but
which works effects in all mental regions
connected with it, effects of so small intensity,
of such rapidly shifting content, that there is
little of it but the vagueness of an aurora.
The artist cannot undervalue even the effects
of admiration of his own skill; for though
the pleasure gained thus is for a few, and
perhaps only for his fellow-workers, for them
it is not a small pleasure-giving element, and
if his work holds the admirer by this means
but a moment longer, so much the more is
that work effective.

Breadth of field without the emphasis of
foci implies a widely divided attention which
it is important for us to consider. The
recognition of the existence of a field in
the percipient lacking in definiteness of attention has, indeed, not infrequently led to
over-emphasis of the receptive state, of the
passive conditions, for art effect; too little

account being taken of the reactive elements involved. These latter, however, do, in fact, make up a large part of the æsthetic complex, as our later æstheticians, Sully, Guyau, and others, do not fail to recognize distinctly. Guyau, in fact, in his zeal to force the recognition of his view, makes himself appear, some will doubtless think, to take an extreme view on the other side, — to over-emphasize the active element.

Any work of art which tends to raise a marked attention in one line necessarily excludes pleasurable psychoses in other lines, in that it lowers the effect of these other presentations or revivals as components of consciousness at the time. A work of art, in which the elements are so balanced that the observer is kept in a state of nicely divided and still of constantly shifting pleasurable attention, will produce the most widespread, the most voluminous, even though not the most vivid, pleasure.

The power of music is often clearly aided

N

by its indefiniteness, its "dreaminess," as we call it; and it seems to me that the great strength of the masters of music has lain in their ability to widen the field of pleasure by the means under consideration. In such a complex art as the opera, the difficulty of reaching this balance is very great. An operatic composer of inferior power will not be able to prevent a frequent diversion of attention with consequent loss of fulness. Now one finds one's self watching the stage effects to the exclusion of the music, and again listening to the music with closed eyes, with no thought of the action. In the impression obtained from the best work, some of Wagner's, for instance, I find myself, on the other hand, very often lost in the totality. All particulars seem to be forgotten in the general effect; the stage actions are not separately emphatic; the suggestion to note distinctly the "motifs" is an intrusion. The crudeness in respect to finer play of thought and emotion, which the *plot* in his operas shows, is probably necessary to their power. The strong development of "plot interest" would doubtless act as a detriment to the wide totality.

It is, perhaps, in part the unconscious recognition of this principle of diffusion of attention which leads to the popular opinion that the critical spirit is fatal to æsthetic receptivity; and in one sense this is true, although I am free to confess to the belief that what is lost to the critic in width of field by the concentration of the critical view is largely gained in the region of intellectual play. To the critic who knows his subject well this actually prevents his satiety, overcomes the danger of distaste for works with which he must be over-familiar, although, perhaps, communication of his thought to others less well equipped may in some cases mar their pleasure, by reducing the breadth of pleasure-field, without compensation in other directions.

But width of field has its dangers too, for it makes easy the shifting of one's thought upon lines of pain-giving. An example of this has already been given in another connection, where I called attention to the fact that the tone of voice, or anything which indicates the animus of the describer or critic, will frequently change an æsthetic into a non-æsthetic object for the listener; and *vice versâ.*

The æsthetic state of mind, although largely a matter of the complex summation of vague pleasures, involves more than this. To perfection of art there must exist decided centres of interest, flitting more or less lightly over this vaguer field. To the consideration of this point we now turn.

The Shifting Focus. — In *Amiel's Journal,* 23d May, 1863, we read: " All that is diffused and indistinct, without form or sex or accent, is antagonistic to beauty, for the mind's first need is light. Light means order; and order means, in the first place, the distinction of the parts, in the second, their regular action.

Beauty is based on reason." Although we have seen that exclusively rationalistic views of æsthetics are not tenable, we cannot help agreeing that an object which presents no *virile* interests, but merely a field of moderate pleasures, soon cloys. It becomes "sweet," as they say in the studio. It was probably the recognition of this fact that led Lotze to the theory that beauty requires the grasp of the ideal through some *definite* object, and Volkmann to separate the art field from the field of æsthetics, on the ground that the former strikes a definite chord above the merely hedonic field of æsthetics. For Volkmann this definiteness, which most emphatically takes its object out of its environment, is the direction in which the art of the ancients showed its highest superiority.

But if art work must impress us by its force of attention, its centres of interest, these points of intenser activity are points of danger; all pleasures are ephemeral, the more so as they gain in vividness, and the *shifting* of these centres of interest is of as great importance as their existence. I think we shall find this recognized in certain general principles.

First, we may expect to find means adopted to retain pleasure *in one special direction* by arranging to shift attention away from the special field before us before pain or complete indifference occurs, and back again at the moment when pleasurable recurrence of the content is again possible. This brings before us the great principle of *rhythm.*

Because processes of nutrition are relatively regular, the times required for complete recovery after full use remain approximately equal in the same set of organs, and it thus happens that we learn to. act at recurrent regular intervals, being thus enabled to hold to a special subject-matter for a long time, not only without fatigue, but, if the rhythm be properly timed, with marked pleasure.

Accurate rhythms are most notable in music and poetry, but what may be termed inaccurate rhythms are the very ordinary tools of the artist in other lines also. The power of order, in architecture, for example, and the value of symmetries generally, depend largely upon such rhythms. Instances will be recalled by the reader in all the arts without special example.

Passing to the consideration of the shifting of attention *beyond the same field*, from field to field, we obtain the well-recognized canon of *variety*. Monotony of stimulations gives us first indifference and then the positive pains of fatigue. If the elements of consciousness be constantly changed, however, the chances of pleasure gain are greatly increased; if a unity be recognized in the variety, on the principles already discussed, we have an added pleasure to that gained by the shifting of the centre of interest.

Variety, however, like all the means of pleasure stimulation, is likely to be carried too far. Variety of pleasurable stimulation is exhaustive and will eventually aggravate the

trouble we attempt to correct, by making painful *every* activity in our field. An example
of this we may all recall in the craving for
total rest experienced after a visit to some
great exhibition where competitors vie with
each other to attract attention to their wares
by varied devices looking to pleasure-giving.
We often find people remarking that they
enjoy an art work (especially is this true in
architectural criticism) because it is *simple*.
The distracting elements in the varied objects
which they have examined in the hope of
gaining pleasurable effects have disappeared,
and have left a quiet delight not far removed
from the so-called "pleasures of rest."

Contrasts, already discussed, also gain their
effects through change of region of stimulation. Where notable, however, they depend
upon vividness (hypernormality of action) for
their results, and must be used with care lest
they act exhaustively.

The same thing may be said of those vivid
elements of novelty which give the value to

what we call the picturesque. We cannot use these means to gain æsthetic result unless we are able to turn ourselves away from their stimulation as soon as we begin to be weary. Hence, we should avoid the use of the picturesque in our homes, and should deal most carefully with strong contrasts in the decoration of rooms in which we wish to live, or in buildings which one is compelled to view constantly.

On the whole, it appears that the safest means of producing lasting æsthetic results will be reached if we choose that succession of elements, each of which is naturally led up to by those which have preceded : or to put this in physiological language ; we will gain our result best if we choose such successive impressions as will stimulate organs that have been best and fully prepared for action by the associative nutrition (if I may so speak) connected with the previously stimulated activities.

From this we may argue to a wide æsthetic law, which may perhaps be called the *princi-*

ple of the satisfaction of expectancies — a legitimate description of the means of gaining
æsthetic result here touched upon, as all such
movements of thought appear in retrospect to
be expectation phases which are fulfilled.
That this canon, however, although of wide
application, is not a universal one for æsthetics is apparent when we consider that our
normal, indifferent, scarcely conscious life is
largely made up of these fulfilments of expectation, although not recognized as such, to
be sure, unless their legitimacy is questioned
in one way or another.

In general, then, it appears that the great
artist is one who is able to make use of the
principles above enumerated. Having avoided
pains, having created his wide field of non-
pain, he produces a wide summation of pleasurable elements. Further, he so arranges the
shifting of attention that as one impression
fails in pleasure-giving, another equally enjoyable appears, through natural connection, to

supply the place of that pleasure which is fading away. Moreover, by compelling a judicious recurrence of special interests, he marks a unity of the manifold, which unity gives to his work a distinctive character.

I have already named the great works of Wagner in illustration of the poise of attention; but Wagner's power goes beyond this: wherever we break away from width of effect and allow our attention to concentrate itself upon details, we there find a gem of melody, a delicious progression, a richness of harmony, or a masterful bit of orchestration; and if we turn from the music we are still thrilled with emotion or impressed by some profundity of thought. But withal, these details are not allowed to efface the value of the special marked development of the work. Shakespeare's wonderful drama, to take another example, shows us great width of interest, yet always some figures of *special* interest, from one to the other of which our attention is artfully shifted without loss of that background of delight which is felt apart from the specially forceful impressions. His genius manifests itself further in the ability to preserve a proper balance, so that using wealth of subordinate elements, no one of them is allowed to rise to sufficiently great importance to mar the general movement of the drama, or to detract from the importance of the character whose action is to thrill our souls. The great painter treats his subject in like manner; he gives us a wide, vague, pleasurable background in impression or associative revival trains; a wide field of more marked pleasures over which the centre of interest shifts, without loss of the prominence of the central "motif" to which especially he would compel our recurrence.

It must be apparent to my reader that if capacity to produce relative *permanency* of pleasure be determined by this shifting of points of interest over wide fields of moderate pleasure, then the arts involving the stimulation of successive mental states have a great advantage over those which are dependent upon simple unchanging impression; and on that account, in my view, the arts of literature and of music, and of combinations of the two, must be held to be the arts of pre-eminent importance to-day, and the ones that are likely to become more and more influential as civilization advances.

In bringing to an end this chapter and this book I wish to note a few points concerning the subjects discussed in what has preceded this. In the first and second chapters we studied the nature of the æsthetic effect in the observer; in the third chapter we studied the nature of the impulse that compels the artist to undertake his work; and in the fourth chapter we considered the nature of the critical act and of the standards used when we assume the critical attitude.

The negative and positive principles that we have just been considering have very different worth for us as artists and as observers.

As artists the negative principles, and all the investigations in reference to æsthetic problems that science can make for us, must be of great value as warnings which will help us to avoid the failures experienced by those who have preceded us in the search for beauty. The experience of our race in the past has left record of its failures in certain general negative principles to which we ,cannot but listen; and science we may hope, teaching us by more accurate method, will in the future guide the artist with a surer hand to avoid the pitfalls into which his blind enthusiasm is liable to lead him.

The positive principles aid the artist much less definitely, for, as we have seen, he must depend upon the individual force of the racial instinct within him that guides his artistic expression; so that in practice even these positive principles which we have enumerated must come to be used by him negatively as safeguards against excesses.

When we become observers and critics,

however, we find that the positive and negative principles are more equal in value for
us ; and I wish now to ask my reader in
closing to take up with me the consideration
of a practical problem in criticism which will
illustrate the relative value of these positive
and negative æsthetic principles, and which
will indicate the complication of the subjects
with which a philosophic æsthetic has to deal.
I choose for this purpose the much-discussed
question as to the values of structural form in
architecture.

The study of the development of æsthetics
teaches us that architecture as a fine art has
arisen in the past by the studied attempt to
attach æsthetic qualities to certain settled and
well-understood constructional forms: but
for the discovery of, and the perfecting of,
the constructional methods involved there
could be no architecture. But the mere consideration of these methods has not made
architecture a fine art until the race has
learned to use these constructional tools in

ways that produce within us a sense of beauty.

Now what has in the past been a matter of almost spontaneous and thoroughly racial development we are attempting to make individual and that by rational means. We are attempting to do in our lives by forethought what in the past has been worked out by slow processes of racial effort and by the elimination of the inferior in racial product.

It is clear that we should learn from the history of the subject that structure is of the essence of architecture; that building methods are the *tools* of the artist in this direction; that if he do not use structure as his tool the artist is no architect, although perhaps in some other way he may illumine the field of art; *e.g.*, as a decorator.

But, on the other hand, it must never be forgotten that this structure is *merely* his tool, and that the end to be attained by the architect as well as by any artist is the production of beauty of a special type.

Now we find men crying out that emphasis of structure is all important, and they point to the virile Gothic of France and try to make it teach us that we should treat architecture as the decoration of a skeleton in which bone and sinew should always be prominent; and on the other hand, we find others who, repelled by such views, point to the glories of the palaces of Venice and of the loggias of Florence, and tell us that structural power has little or nothing to do with architectural values.

But I think we may find the truth in a combination of these two opposing views if we bear in mind what has been said above,— that structure is the tool of the architect-artist and that the production of beauty is his goal. He must learn, as his racial prototypes have done, to know thoroughly the settled principles of construction, so that he may be able to *think* in structural forms; so that the arches, the roofs, etc., that he sketches may be constructed practically as he sketches them.

o

For the most part, the use of these structural tools involves negative æsthetic principles only. It is, as we have seen, a negative principle of the greatest moment that the artist should avoid shocks, and surely if in his design the architect bring into prominence the perception of any active constructional force he ought also to leave unmasked the counter force that holds the former in equilibrium; otherwise he will leave with us a sense of unrest that is distinctly subversive of æsthetic effect.

From a positive æsthetic standpoint there is this to note, that for the average highly cultivated man it is a distinct gain to bring out clearly the constructional conception, provided this can be done without destroying other beauty of a higher order; but the production of this beauty is the architect's goal, and he surely will show himself a mere builder and no artist if in his emphasis of the structure he lose higher æsthetic qualities. If, however, he be a master and be able to mark the structural elements without loss, or even with gain, to the beauty of the whole, he will add a new source of delight to his work which will be of great value.

Now to turn to an opposite effect, namely, the use of structural forms as mere decorative features; such work as we find in all modern Renaissance architecture which gains its inspiration, in this respect, from the Romans, who called in the Greeks to face their constructional skeletons with Greek-like decorative architectural robes.

If this use of structural forms of the past involves recognizable pretence of structural use, where such use does not exist, there rings out a false note in the scheme; there is a violation of our negative canon which tells us to *avoid untruth*, because untruth gives a shock which is fatal to beauty. But on the other hand, if those forms of structural decoration make no pretence to have structural values, and are in themselves beautiful (as, by the way, many of the modern Renaissance details are *not*), and if by their use the proportions or colour masses of the building may be brought into more harmonious relation than were otherwise possible, or if in other respects the building be thereby beautified, I can see no critical objection whatever to their use. The most that can be said against such ornament is that in its use we confess our lack of vigorous, true, architectural genius; and that such use tends to make us decorators and not architects, and leads to a loss of deep architectural conviction.

Speaking *negatively* again, the architect should use his structural tools economically, so that we may not be oppressed by any valueless expenditure of human time and effort; but on the other hand *positively*, it is perfectly valid for him to use unneeded flesh (so to speak) to cover his structural skeleton, where it is plain and evident that the super-fluous material and labour is employed for the legitimate special purpose of adding to the æsthetic effectiveness of the whole.

Thus while the architect must use his tools rationally to avoid offence, and if he be a genius may be able to use these very tools as effective æsthetic instruments, he must never forget that the end in view is the attainment of beauty.

And here we have an interesting example of one of the main principles I above defend. As I have said before, we cast out beyond the boundaries of the æsthetic all that pains, but we do not necessarily call a total work unæsthetic because it contains painful elements, provided it also contains sufficient of beauty to overwhelm with satisfactions the minor discords.

So one who has become steeped with the beauty of the masterpieces of French Gothic, with their emphasis of structural elements, must often experience a sense of loss when he views the works of the early Tuscan masters; but notwithstanding the minor discords in this work produced by structural ineffectiveness, the superabundant beauty of proportion and

detail and colour compel within him a deep
satisfaction that the sombre might of Amiens
or Beauvais cannot produce.   And then turn
to the glory of the best Greek work where
this constructional discord is lacking; where
the structure indeed tells its historic story and
unostentatiously speaks of its strength; and
where withal, above all, stands emphatic that
sense of perfected beauty of line and propor-
tioned colour mass which leads us to bow
before the masters who thus surpassed us.
There we have true architectural beauty of
the highest type.

THE END.

INDEX.

Pain, Pleasure, and Æsthetics.

BY

HENRY RUTGERS MARSHALL.

Cloth. 8vo. $3.00.

MACMILLAN & CO.,

66 FIFTH AVENUE, NEW YORK.

LaVergne, TN USA
21 January 2010
170795LV00006B/95/A